senses of architecture

using the senses to enhance architectural experience

BIS Publishers
Timorplein 46
1094 CC Amsterdam
The Netherlands
T +31 (0)20 515 02 30
bis@bispublishers.com
www.bispublishers.com

ISBN 978 90 636 9724 2

senses of architecture

using the senses to enhance architectural experience

Ryan Crooks

Hand Drawings by
Constanza Loustalet

BISPUBLISHERS

Table of Contents

Design and the Senses

The senses play a crucial role in how we experience the world around us, and designers can use these experiences to their advantage when creating products and experiences. By carefully considering how the senses can be engaged, designers can create more immersive and provoking designs that are effective at capturing the user's attention and interest.

One of the most important senses in design is vision. Visual elements, such as color, shape, and texture, can be used to create a visually appealing design that captures the user's attention and draws them in. In addition, visual hierarchy, which refers to the arrangement of visual elements in a design, can be used to direct the user's attention and guide them through the design.

Another important sense in design is hearing. Auditory elements, such as music, sound effects, and voiceovers, can be used to create a more captivating and immersive experience for the user. For example, the use of a dynamic and interesting soundtrack can help to set the tone for a design and create a more extensive experience.

In addition to vision and hearing, other senses, such as touch and smell, can also be used in design to create a more holistic and multi-sensory experience. For example, the use of haptic feedback, such as vibrations or other textured surfaces, can help to make a design more interactive and inviting. Similarly, the use of scents in various forms can help to create a more immersive and memorable experience for the user.

Overall, the senses play a crucial role in how we experience the world around us. Really, the senses are the only way we are able to know the external world, and designers can use this to their advantage when creating products and spaces. By carefully considering how the senses can be engaged and used in design, designers can create more effective and engaging designs that are more successful at capturing the user's attention and interest.

Target Audience

This work's target audience is architects and designers with the desire to heighten the impact of design through the use of and interaction with our senses. Although designers typically explore through vision, structures and spaces can become more complex through the addition of various combinations of our twenty or more senses. We know the traditional five senses, but there are others, and touch can be divided into several senses. The interaction with the various forms of our senses will make not only the building or place richer, but ourselves as well.

The interested and knowledgeable user or visitor may also gain clues how to glean sensory experience from a space, especially as more designers begin to use the other senses in their work. Furthermore, this work can be a guide to help clients suggest sensory design ideas to their architects and interior designers.

What is the purpose of this book?
This work prods the designer to awaken the dormant senses in design that have been ignored and surely atrophied through neglect when interacting with a space. For too long, we have consumed what buildings and places look like, imagery and details showing only how the structures and spaces appear, not feel like, not sound like, not smell like. This imagery likely only provides a superficial understanding of a location or object. To learn and understand with our various forms of touch, smell, hearing, and even taste in some instances, ensures we have a more comprehensive knowledge of an object or space. With increased knowledge, the designer and user can create or find a better definition or understanding of the object or space, which allows a new possibility for it.

What does this do for the reader?
This work provides a basic description of the various senses, and it also gives understanding, interpretation, and modes of use for these senses to allow the reader to create deeper, more sensory designs. The depth of the senses promotes a better experiential space. Further, a section of this work illustrates ways to map and annotate the proposed senses and their use in both the design and document phases in order to convey the intent to those constructing and reviewing the work. Beyond this, the work provides possible and practical ways to introduce the senses, as well as possible combinations of senses as outputs and inputs using electronics.

Although some of this book might be new or surprising, it is meant to be a practical work that spurs the designer to explore design and the senses in the world beyond an abstract book and theory. Really, the use of the various senses creates a more concrete understanding of the space, design, and even the designer.

What are comparable titles and how do these books differ?
Although we have many senses, most design is focused on the visual. Some forms of design explore sound, but the other senses are generally ignored. This is reflected in available design literature, which has very few titles and articles that explore all or most of the senses in design. There is an ever-growing body of knowledge on the senses in the sciences, but it is exactly that: knowledge, but much or most of it does not look at how to use the sciences as a tool for the designer, and not really for other fields, such as engineering. This might be because of the moral and ethical considerations of using people for study and experimentation, and it is understood that if used poorly, design and the senses could cause discomfort and possibly pain in some cases. This work does not discuss nor promote certain ways the senses can hurt the individual. In any case, much of the limited printed design material available is provided in the resources section of this book, however it is surprising how sparse this subject is in architecture and interior design, especially because the way design is promoted in school is as a very experiential field.

The Author
Ryan Henderson Crooks is an architect and educator who has practiced and taught architecture and interior design for over twenty years. He designs and develops work throughout the United States, as well as several countries around the world. Ryan's practice explores our existence in a changing world and attempts to improve conditions through the built environment. Ryan Crooks also designs solar energy plants, as well as storage systems, to provide electricity across the United States' energy grids. Ryan has won several awards for his work, has written many articles and two books about architecture, design methods, and materials.

The Senses in Design

As a designer or architect, we must understand who the user is and then what is the program, or what is to be designed before we begin the sensory design. It would be good to have an interview with the client or a sample user to have a perspective and wants. Once this is understood, the designer must provide a thesis, theme, or parti. This will define how the project will be designed for the user. There are so many ways a single design can be completed that the architect and designer must determine the constraints and ways to measure the quality and effectiveness of the design. Once these items are determined, the senses can be chosen.

Having the program, knowledge of the user, and the thesis or theme, we must ask how the user will experience the idea of the project. What is experience, but the interpretation of the physical interaction with the environment. This physical interaction is through the use of the senses. Of course, we can count on the reliable sense of vision, but we should look beyond vision to find ways to express the main idea of the project. There are at least twenty senses including hearing, touch, smell, taste, and vision, but also other senses such as proprioception, equilibrioception, and the sense of time. Which senses are best to convey the point of the design? Each sense provides information and experience in a different way, and it is important for the designer and architect to know the differences between each.

When designing, do not start with the visual. The sense of vision is constantly being used. Really, it is too heavily used in design. In fact, for a strong sensory experience, the visual should be the last sense to be reviewed and designed for. Instead, examine the thesis, then the program and user, and select a typically secondary sense, such as hearing or touch, or to make an especially innovative space or object, start with smell, taste, or even chemoreception in order to begin the design.

Each sense has its advantages, and each one is different, and they are not interchangeable. In this way, use the information from or activation of one sense for only that sense – do not use the same meaning or experience for multiple senses, only one. This is to provide variation and complexity in the overall design. We do not want the monotony of one stimulus across multiple senses, creating a flat, single dimensional space. From this, we understand that the designer can and should use multiple senses, each in its own way.

Write down which senses are to be used, then the mode of the experience must be determined. For each sense, define if it is active, using technology, or if it is passive, using materials and objects that are not electronic or electrical. For example, a designer can provide a scent by actively spraying a perfume with a machine every ten minutes, or an object can be infused with the oils and scent, or even better, the object can be the origin of the scent. In this example, we could have an atomizer spray cinnamon scent periodically, have a wood or paper surface that is anointed with the cinnamon scented oils, or have sticks of cinnamon. Using an atomizer is active, whereas the oils and natural scents are passive.

For the active, we will explore ways to use electronics and hardware to provide the senses in this work, but say it is a passive mode that is desired? What is the object or material that will require or employ a sense? How will that object or material be employed in the design? Is it passive itself, in that the sense experience is placed within the design without control of the output and meaning, like the sound of caged birds, or does the object or material get introduced to the visitor in some way in the exploration of the design? The latter provides more control of how and when the sense is experienced, but it requires more specification and detail on how the sense is used. In fact, it is similar to the active mode in its complexity and need for delineation.

Once the senses and modes of conveyance are determined, the designer must explore the meaning and possible secondary meaning of the chosen senses. Is the meaning, feeling, and experience of the sensory input the same or similar to that desired and expected? Is there a better way to do this? Are there other or expanded meanings when using the sense? Then, what is a side effect or secondary result of using the sense? Finally, reaching beyond the simple or concrete, can the use of the senses make the imperceptible sensed and practical?

When the above items have been answered, we can begin to map out the senses in preliminary and schematic design. In the first pass, the chosen senses should be enumerated, and strategies on how to employ them may be determined. If the method of the senses' use is not yet known, we can revisit this in the design documentation and contract documents phases. In any case, during the preliminary and schematic design phases, the sense experience should be documented with text as notes, annotations, and possibly examples or precedents. The notes may be general, provided on the first pages of the design, but they may already be topical at certain locations in the design. Furthermore, the annotations in the early stages, beyond notes,

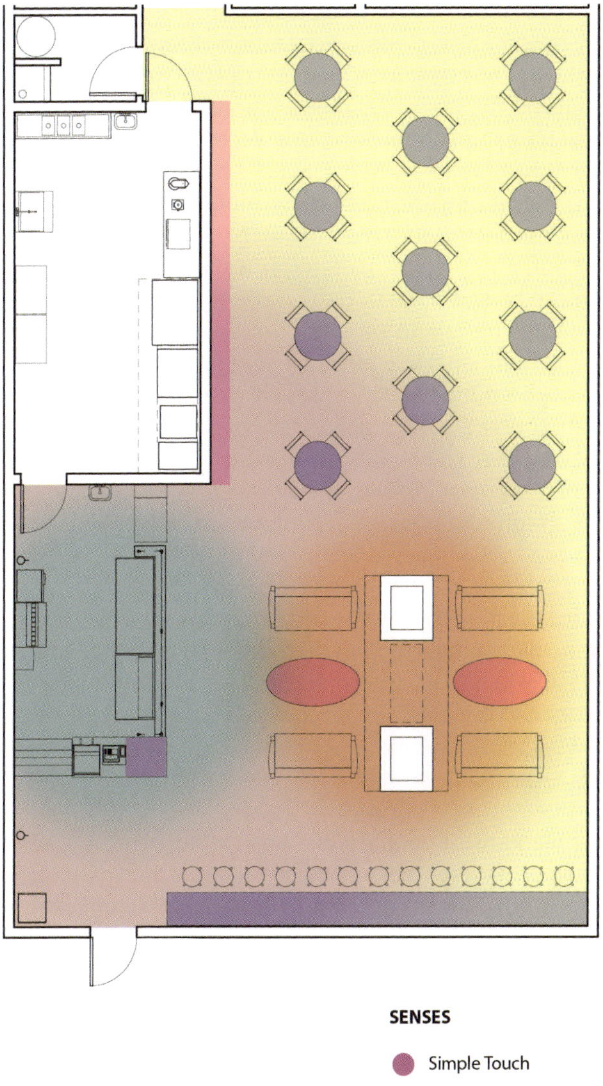

SENSES

- Simple Touch
- Cold Thermoception
- Heat Thermoception
- Sound
- Smell
- Taste

could be leaders to locations in the drawings, providing key information. With multiple passes at the design, a collection of sensory experiences will be curated and the use of a heat map diagram can be used to illustrate location, type, and degree of the senses. Using the standard projections of the project's design is a fine base to mark the locations. Because the use of the senses is meant to add dynamism to a scheme, the designer should feel comfortable using sections, elevations, and three-dimensional drawings, as well as the standard plans, as underlays for the heat map diagram.

Type of sense can be conveyed through color or a symbol for the heat map diagram. We should be careful with the choice of color for the senses, as we may think of the traditional five senses: hearing, touch, smell, taste, and vision, however there are around twenty senses we discuss in this work, with many of them related to touch. So, we might choose five colors for the typical senses, but we might also have color variations for touch, though we need to worry about any conflict in meaning with the degree of the sense and sense color. Alternately, we might use symbols in conjunction with color for the great array of the senses.

Finally, we must diagram the degree or amount of the sense. This can be done in the heat map diagram through the saturation of the color, so lighter equals less of the sense, when using color instead of a symbol. With the use of a symbol, we can use the size of the symbol to denote the amount of the sense used. In this way, a larger symbol would equal a greater amount of the sense used.

The heat map diagram is a very useful drawing to develop and reference in the early stages of design because it illustrates a spatial and experiential quality that is absent with the use of traditional architectural drawings, like plans, sections, elevations, and perspectives. However, we can use additional methods of representation in the design document and contract document phases of design. These additional methods include tags with annotations, schedules, and details.

When designing with the senses, we can introduce a new tag to our drawing set. The geometry of the tag might vary, but we will use a pentagon, because each side represents one of the five traditional senses and because we do not usually use the pentagon for any other tags in architecture. In this way, it does not compete with window, furniture, material, wall, or lighting tags.

Within the pentagon we will use an abbreviated form of the sense and a number. The abbreviation simply marks the sense used, and the number provides which variation or experience is used in the location tagged. In an example, we can use multiple scents in a design, and we would mark the tag with "SM" for smell and a number for the instance, such as "SM1" for citrus in the kitchen and "SM2" for vanilla in the conference room. Here are the suggested abbreviations:

TO Touch
PS Pressure
IT Itch
CO Cold Thermoception
HT Heat Thermoception
PR Proprioception
TE Tension
ST Stretch
VI Vibration
EQ Equilibrioception
SO Sound
TA Taste
SM Smell
CH Chemoreception
TI Time
TH Thirst
HU Hunger
V Vision

These tags can be referenced to another form of documentation common in design: the schedule. The schedule would include all relevant information for the plans and may also refer to additional cutsheets or manufacturer specifications. This list of sensory information would provide, in a compact form that is easy to take in at a single view, much of the necessary description that is not or cannot be described in the drawings, annotations, and tags. Likely columns to include in the sense schedule are:

Tag
Name
Brief Description
Dimensions
Defining Properties (such as Wattage, Solution, or Volume)
Reference to Relevant Details or Cutsheets

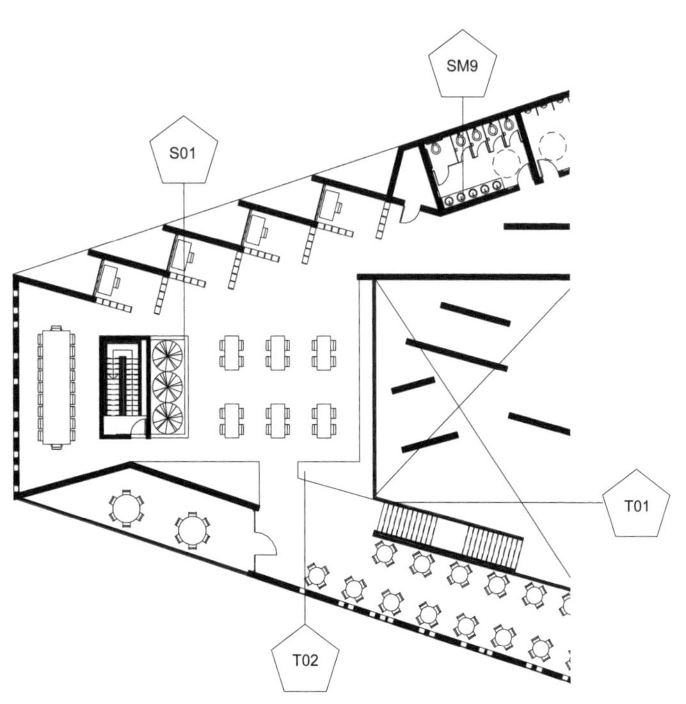

Specialty Equipment Schedule					
Sense Tag	Sense Name	Sense Description	Sense Dimensions	Sense Properties	Sense Reference
SM9		Scent from hand soap and cleaning products	Liquid; varies	Materials provided through custodian and site manager	4/A513
SO1	Running Water	Water feature in planter provides aural highlight	24"x36"x14"	12V Motor; Water and Container	23/A508
TO1	Hand Rail Pattern	Texture marks the beginning of the stairs	4 Linear Feet	Machined handrail	4/A10
TO2	Seating Cushioning Pattern	Pattern of stitching and cushioning create textural interest for visitors	48"x48"x4"	Upholstery	12/A10

Beyond the schedule, we would have the details of the sense experience, which would provide material and dimensional information about the assemblage of the experience through traditional orthographic projections and three-dimensional drawings. A sensory experience may have only one detail needed to explain the design, or it may have several, depending on the complexity and abstraction of the design. We should be aware that drawings are useful for design but not everything can be conveyed through two-dimensional constructions on a drawing sheet: models, prototypes, and precedent objects may be helpful. In conjunction with the drawings and representations, the details, schedules, and tags with annotations should provide enough information for the contractor or consultant to understand how to construct and install the sense designs.

Passive versus Active

When the senses are documented in the preliminary, schematic, design development, and contract document phases, the designer must determine whether the sensory experiences are passive or active. If they are passive, then the documentation provided in the contract documents and cut sheets is adequate to define the design. However, if the experiences are active, requiring electric or electronic design, then the method, hardware, and software necessary to achieve the sense moment must be defined for each experience.

In a design installation, we will assume that there are many sensory experiences, but how many using electronics are there? We must provide a precise number and determine where each of these is located. The drawings and diagrams, as mentioned above, will be able to provide the location, and we can simply count the number of active sense moments given in the drawings, if adequately annotated. If the drawings do not have a designation for active experiences, then it will be useful to do so with addenda and supporting documents to avoid contractor requests for information and change orders.

After counting the number of active sense moments to design for, the designer should divide and separate these into the various senses, in order to provide structure for the design and documentation. In fact, the details should be separated by sense per sheet in order to allow the various designs to share notes and specifications when necessary. So, all smell designs are on a sheet, all hearing designs are on another sheet, et cetera.

Next, we must evaluate how we are going to use these individual moments. There are many ways we can do this, including mapping a sense input to another sense output, translating the input to another, more understandable meaning, and providing a sense response to some stimulus. Really, there are countless ways to use the senses, but the structure of these sense experiences can be broken down to just a handful, really only five, relationships of cause and effect.

We will go over these five relationships, but in order to do so, we need to understand what the sensory input and the sensory output are, or what is the cause and effect? In the way we interact with the world, everything we experience is a form of sensory input. Language, data, sounds, touch, imagery, tastes: everything that we perceive comes into our brains through some sense. We must define what is the precise sense we will focus on as the input for each experience, and from this we can develop the relationship that will lead the cause (input) to the effect (output).

When determining the sensory input, we must define the sensory output. What is supposed to happen? Is there some smell that wafts through the space? Does a surface go from smooth to rippled? Do the acoustics of the space change? It is crucial to define this output in order to put together the interrelation of cause and effect. As the designer, there should be a clear and definite outcome, aligning with the design intentions.

Once we have the input, output, and relationship between the two, we can analyze the cause and effect relationship and develop a conditional statement to describe the interactivity between the two. This conditional statement in everyday speech will be similar to: if something, then something else. The script to define this conditional statement to the microcontroller or computer looks very similar with a little different syntax.

There can be a very simple relationship defined by a simple conditional statement, or it can be a more complex relationship where certain values make specific things happen or not happen, while others provide alternate experiences. In this way, we can define the five different relationships we are able to use to program the electronics and hardware for the sense experience. Toward the end of this book, there is a brief description of each as well as script examples for each. However, the following is a preview of the relationships.

The first relationship is binary mapping. This is one of the simpler relationships where an input provides one output. It is off or on, there is no other option in this relationship. An example of this is to express a citrus scent when a sensor sees the color orange.

The next relationship is one-to-one. Really, this relationship can be considered two relationships in that the input and output are related to one another but with different results. The first one-to-one relationship is the direct relationship where a sense experience increases with the increase of the sense input. An example of this would be a space growing brighter with more noise. Counter to this relationship, there is the indirect one-to-one relationship. In this, the sense experience decreases as the input increases, and the experience increases as the input decreases. If we continue with the same example, in an indirect one-to-one relationship, a space would grow darker with more noise, and the space would become brighter with less noise.

Next, we have the threshold relationship, which is somewhat like the combination of the binary with the one-to-one relationship. When using a threshold conditional statement, a sense experience will occur when a certain value or amount of the sense input is present. For example, music might play when there are seven or more people in a space.

Finally, we have multiple thresholds, which is a relationship that determines the amount of sensory input and provides different outputs, depending on the input values. For this condition, the threshold example above can be expanded to the type of music being dependent on the number of people in the space. So, soft piano music will play for seven to fifteen people present, brass music will play for sixteen to thirty, and club music will play for more than thirty people present.

These are the five relationships, but the interaction of the sensory inputs and outputs can become more complex with the combination of these. Furthermore, it is possible to add even more dynamism with the introduction of more than one input, output, and conditional statement to a design moment. However, you might find it is better to keep the interaction spare and limited to avoid sensory overload.

In order to program the sense experience, we can use special hardware and software that is accessible to the designer. There are several user-ready options available, and one of the most popular is Arduino. Arduino consists of a programmable circuit board, which is also called a microcontroller, and software, which is also called an Integrated Development Environment (IDE). The designer uses the software (IDE) to program the microcontroller to perform certain tasks. In combination with these, there are various sensors and actuators which mimic or extend our own senses and physical abilities. Many examples of these are provided in the overviews of each of the senses later in this work.

For active sensory design using the microcontroller, we have discussed conditional statements that describe actions that occur from some sensory cause. The sensors are the input, and the microcontroller reads the values provided by the sensor. These readings are always a number in a specific range. The designer can use these numbers in the conditional statement to set up how the microcontroller translates this information, whether it is binary, one-to-one direct, one-to-one indirect, a threshold, or thresholds. Then, some actuator performs a task given in the conditional statement when the requirements have been met. The effect can be a sensory stimulus, such as heat, sound, change of texture, or it can be physical movement, using motors and similar. These three parts make up the active design, and if the designer is thoughtful and attentive to the user's experience, then the use of technology will create a dynamic and interactive sensory moment.

The coding used in Arduino's IDE is based on Processing, a language created for artists and designers. This is a very simple but powerful language which allows anyone to program hardware with script that is easily understandable and applicable. The scripts, which are called sketches for Arduino, have the conditional statements described above, but they also define how the sensors and actuators communicate with the microcontroller, which is usually through pins on the board. The pins have different functionality on the Arduino microcontroller, but most can both receive data and transmit data using low voltage signals and power width modulation.

Because the Arduino is so popular, with a reasonably long history, we are able to see and use other people's sketches to learn new functionality and interfaces with hardware and other software. In fact, the Arduino community is rather open, and it is possible for the designer to use new and surprising features and scripts developed, as long as the designer gives attribution. Unlike some other microcontrollers and systems, Arduino allows users to share and grow knowledge without risk of interfering in others' intellectual property. However, Arduino is not the only system like this; other systems include BeagleBoard, Teensy, and Launchpad. Nevertheless, for the purposes of this work, we will use Arduino.

The Arduino can be very fast to program and test, and it is critical that the designer follow the typical design process:

Define the Problem
Develop a Solution
Create a Prototype
Test the Solution
Evaluate the Results
Repeat until the Results Meet the Expectations

Defining the problem is very much as described earlier: what does the designer want to accomplish? What senses will be used for the input and output or cause and effect?

In order to develop a solution, the designer must create a conditional statement to relate the input or cause with the output or effect. Furthermore, the designer must define the interaction: binary, one-to-one direct or indirect, a threshold, or thresholds.

Creating the prototype is relatively simple with the Arduino microcontroller and IDE, and nearly all sensors and actuators will work with the Arduino environment. This hardware is readily available on the internet or at some hobby and electronics stores. Also, because Arduino is so popular, it is likely that the hardware has been used before, and the sketch with the programming script could very easily be available online. If not, the community is very helpful and will likely be able to provide answers and solutions on how to program and assemble the prototype.

When testing the solution, the designer should first remember the design intent. Then, the prototype can be tested and judged with specific criteria set forth by the designer. Ultimately, is the solution able to provide the interaction and sensory experience initially desired? If not, try again. Sometimes, we must change the intent to meet the possibilities, if our initial intent is not an option for some reason. However, this is the last resort, and it is better to run through the design process several times to hone in on the solution. Design is a reiterative task.

Possible Senses per Program

	Lobby	Corridor	Restroom	Office	Classroom	Lecture Hall	Meeting	Library	Café	Janitor's Closet	Patient Room	Surgery	Nurse's Station	Kitchen
Touch	•	•	•									•		
Pressure		•			•							•		
Itch											•	•	•	
Cold	•		•	•					•					
Heat	•			•					•					
Proprioception	•	•			•	•	•			•		•		
Tension		•					•				•		•	
Stretch		•					•				•		•	
Vibration	•	•					•	•						
Nociception											•	•	•	
Equilibrioception		•				•		•						
Sound	•		•	•	•	•		•	•		•			
Taste									•					•
Smell	•		•	•					•					•
Chemoreception												•		•
Time			•	•	•			•	•	•		•		•
Thirst									•					•
Hunger									•					•
Magnetoreception		•						•						
Vision	•			•	•	•				•	•			•

	Gallery	Greenhouse	Tool Shed	Studio	Library	Print Room	Garage	Pharmacy	Closet	Clothing Retail	Electronics Retail	Market	Playground	Movie Theater
Touch		•	•	•	•	•		•	•	•	•	•	•	•
Pressure			•				•	•	•				•	•
Itch								•						
Cold	•			•				•		•		•		
Heat	•			•				•		•		•		
Proprioception				•	•		•		•	•	•	•	•	•
Tension			•	•				•					•	
Stretch			•	•									•	
Vibration	•		•		•						•		•	•
Nociception			•					•						
Equilibrioception	•			•	•		•			•	•	•	•	•
Sound	•	•		•	•	•	•	•			•	•	•	•
Taste												•		
Smell		•	•	•		•	•		•	•		•	•	•
Chemoreception								•				•		
Time		•		•		•					•	•		•
Thirst												•		
Hunger												•		
Magnetoreception					•		•							
Vision	•			•		•				•	•	•		•

Design Combinations

Elements of Design

Shape
Color
Tone
Space
Form
Line
Value
Texture

Principles of Design

Emphasis
Balance
Alignment
Contrast
Repetition
Proportion
Movement
Negative Space
Variety
Hierarchy
Rhythm
Pattern
Unity
Harmony

using

Senses

Simple Touch
Pressure
Itch
Cold Thermoception
Heat Thermoception
Proprioception
Tension
Stretch
Vibration
Equilibrioception
Sound
Smell
Taste
Hunger
Thirst
Chemoreception
Time
Vision

Telling a Story with the Senses

In design and architecture, we use the senses to communicate.

Use should be localized, not pervasive.

The baseline is no sensory stimulus.

When using sensory input, emphasize no more than three senses.

Variation is best within a sensory theme.

Use sensory input lightly, then build up the stimulus as needed.

Sensory response is based in culture: results may vary by group and location.

Appeal to the user, not to your own interests.

Don't allow the cliche or motif to be your first choice.

Simplify your use of the senses – not every element needs to be highlighted with sensory input.

Challenge the user through sensory experience – are there new combinations or possibilities? New Experience = Memory & Impact

Analyze sensory experiences that have moved you. Can you use similar ones in your project?

Make a list of moments and plot turns. Then, apply sense experiences to them. Then, do it again – your first choice probably won't be your best – let the experience be surprising.

Take a position on your sensory use – what you choose can do more than simply affect a sense.

Ensure that your story is worth telling – try not to just use the senses as a gimmick.

Allow others to test your scheme before the final installation – are you communicating what you intended?

If your work is not exactly as intended, readjust and save any ideas for another time.

Take an experience you didn't like and imagine how it could be improved with the senses.

Try to allow your sensory experiences to change the actions of the user.

What is the simplest way to express the story through the senses? Start with that and see what you can add.

Find the inflection points of the story – use at least these moments to provide sensory experience.

Your story can be contextual or it can be just like a book. What will your story be?

Rags to Riches (Rise)
Riches to Rags (Fall)
Man in a Well (Fall > Rise)
Icarus (Rise > Fall)
Cinderella (Rise > Fall > Rise)
Oedipus (Fall > Rise > Fall)

Sensory Example I

Doctor's office needs a design to calm patients with touch, smell, or hearing.

In this example we understand the location as an office or institutional-like space with seating, hard surfaces, and a staff that may be removed from the patients. The senses selected can have different solutions, and a combination of the chosen senses is open.

For touch, we want something that is comforting, reassuring, and personal, although it needs to be easy to clean and re-use. With touch, we can use pressure that reassures, and this can be employed in the furniture. The chair or sofa can be welcoming and positive with enough cushioning and careful curves, folds, and creases to accommodate the human body. Another option is a soothing material, such as a sheer fabric. Can this fabric be easily cleaned and re-used? Yes, a synthetic fabric could work well for this. There are other options for touch that we will look at later in this work.

Using smell, we would like something that is subtle and does not remind someone of healthcare facilities, cleaning, or something too sharp. Many perfume and soap makers use complex but quiet scents such as earth, grass, or water to comfort people but also not be too intense, being pervasive and ever-present. In combination, there can be occasional scent notes that complement or even contrast with the general smell to enliven a space. The ping of an orange scent at an instance can be like a firework in the night. Or, a vanilla note to pair with the smell of grass can create a wonderful chord like a major triad.

Finally, hearing can meet the design requirement. We may want to deaden the sound in a space, if it is too busy and difficult to speak. However, we may want to add a naturalistic sound that counters the artificial interior–the sound of birds at dawn, wind through grass, or water over stones? Something else? On the other hand, in some instances we might want to heighten the existing, current experience whether to highlight some part of the interior or as entertainment or relief. The sound of paper brushing over paper could be amplified with hard, smooth surfaces. The whirring of motors can be a relaxing background noise. What about the footsteps of the staff or people passing? The steady rhythm and variation of the walkers can create an interesting composition.

There are many options for the case of a doctor's office, trying to calm the patients. Again, one sense that is brought forth in the design is fine, but would it be even better with two or more sensory events, and can they come and go in rhythm? We must try the combinations to find what is best then test it on the users and update as needed.

Sensory Example II

Waiting area at a train station using hearing, touch, and vision.

A city train station fluctuates between extremely busy spells and relatively empty moments. Throughout the day, there is quite a bit of commotion. We can augment this or counter it with our sensory design. We will assume a zone in the waiting area has been set aside for our installation, and let's assume it is an enclosed space. How the enclosure is created, we can worry about later, but let's look at the senses.

We will start with hearing. There is a great deal of noise in a busy train station, so let's first look at limiting this noise with baffling and the introduction of white noise. This noise can be added with a machine or audio track, but we can also use flowing water in the space. Which of these makes the most sense depends on the installation's theme. A train station is very dynamic with manmade machines and spaces, so a waterfall could be an interesting counterpoint. However, we might want to build up the artificial, constructed atmosphere with white noise from a synthesizer, helping elevate the place beyond the natural.

What if we want to continue in this way with noise, but instead of masking the environment, we build it up? If we would like to continue with the synthesizer, we could create an ambient music track or sample another ambiance and broadcast it in the space. Or, we could record and loop with audio effects the hustle and bustle of the station users; there are many other possibilities as well. Again, this all depends on what the design intent is.

Now for touch, a train station is consistently composed of hard materials that do not allow imprint. This makes sense, because the station is meant to be used by thousands of people daily, for decades, and many softer materials will not be able to weather well with repeated and constant use. So, let's counter this with soft materials that show use, as we will assume this installation is temporary, whether for a month or a couple years. Perhaps, the materials of the enclosure itself can be of this soft material. We could use traditional materials and methods, such as velvety textiles or upholstery with padding and fine stitching. But, what if the enclosure used a more contemporary material: maybe we can use air or water. We could create a balloon-like structure that is filled with one of these. Furthermore, if we used either the air or water to fill the enclosure, we might also be able to use it to create the white noise from the hearing section above.

In comparison with the site, we could create a dramatic structure that overaccentuates sharp angles, hard surfaces, and permanence. What if the enclosure and its furnishings were composed of metal – spikes, chains, and hard edges? The choice of material could create a glittering, reflective form that entices the viewer but affronts the one who touches it. Whether we compare or contrast with the context, we must differentiate with it to some extent to call out our space as an event, as something special.

Finally, let's look at how we can use vision. Many train stations rely on natural light throughout the day and artificial light in the nighttime to illuminate the space. So, let's look at augmenting the light for some length, as well as limiting the light for another. First, let's think about blocking the surrounding light with an opaque enclosure. This allows us to create our own light sources, perhaps a light show. This show could vary and change with different types and colors of light – spotlighting, uplighting, and downlighting with different colors and varying intensity. This might be interesting, but it must fit with the idea of the designer. For an enclosure or a space within a site, this is a classic way to differentiate with the surroundings – lighting variation.

What if for the lighting, we want to have the enclosure *be* the lighting? How can light emanate from the structure? Does it glow? If so, maybe the water or air balloon structure above can light up like a toy or lantern. This choice ties the senses together through the design. However, we might want to explore other options, such as LED panels, or structural outlining with led strips similar to what we saw in the White City of the Columbian Exposition or many science fiction movies. This creates an otherworldly ambiance, allowing the structure to be like an alien craft landed in the middle of the station. Again, what is the intent of the designer?

Sensory Example III

Bedroom for a workaholic in an apartment using touch and smell.

This example allows us to look at someone more eccentric than the previous two examples, and we must determine how we want to design for this person. As an architect using sensory design, we do not want to treat the space in a standard, basic way, instead we want to heighten either the experience in the room or accentuate the nature of the user. Really, it can be both, and we will determine this after we have gone through some possibilities.

First, let's look at the context. As an apartment, we understand that there are other living spaces with unrelated users in proximity with this dwelling unit, and they are most likely adjacent with only walls and floors to separate them. In this way, there will always be some interaction among the tenants, and the spaces are likely to transmit noise across the spatial boundaries.

Next, we see that the user is a workaholic. As such, this person does not want to focus on downtime and relaxation, instead work and completion of goals are the main objectives. We do not need to work on making the space more stress-free, unless the user requests this. Instead, as a workaholic, the person wants to continue this path – it is how she or he achieves the highest self. We will meet the user's expectations.

The bedroom is a personal space, but it can also be a location for work and study. By definition, it is a space that has a bed, and the bed is for sleeping and relaxing, but in many buildings, especially apartments, the available space is limited, and the various rooms stretch their program. During the pandemic, living spaces became people's entire worlds, and though we do not want to be shackled to our dwellings, it is clear that we can use these spaces beyond the traditional or typical ways. So, a bedroom can be a place to work, as well as sleep. Do we place a desk or table in the bedroom? Are we going to use the bed as the workspace? If so, how does this happen? We can make any of these choices, and each of them brings more options and opportunities. We will place a table and two chairs in the bedroom, and these can be used for other things, beyond work.

For the senses, first we will look at touch. The workaholic likely does not want any distractions, so we should try to use materials and textiles with regularity, meaning with consistent patterns and weaves, without great variation. This will provide controlled surfaces and a consistent space, but we may want to have a little subversion where the components of these patterns have differences and inconsistencies. This would more than likely require handmade and handworked materials, rather than the consistent, monotonous forms pumped out by a machine.

Where will we use these? The linens, floor, wall surfaces, table, and chairs are all possibilities, and we can explore hard surfaces, such as flooring, stone, and the structural components for the furniture, but we can also use textiles, such as rugs and carpets, coverings for the furniture, and any accoutrements. Let's have matching bed and table coverings, then choose a fabric for the chairs and a separate patterned area rug that are complementary. All of these textiles should not only be regularly patterned and handmade, but also have dimensionality, where the user can touch them and feel the variation. In this variation with small inconsistencies, we will be able to provide enough difference to satisfy this busy person.

Next, with smell, we don't want to overwhelm the user with experiential scents, but we would like to either have a consistency with a low, unobtrusive smell, or more likely, we would like to have small highlights throughout the day. These highlights can come through the user's day to day activities, such as the soap at the sink and in the bath, foods for the various meals of the day, and any floral occasions. Beyond this, we have an opportunity to have caches of scents throughout the user's space, perfumes that are inlaid within the closet, clothing, and linens. We can also choose the detergents for cleaning, and in addition, we might want to have moments of scent like potpourri and lotions. All of these scents should be subtle with small variations to create different experiences when sensed.

These two sensory inputs can be used alone, but it would be better to use both to create a more dynamic environment. Again, the experiences should be minimally invasive, but clearly extant.

Sensory Example IV

Trending clothing retailer floor area using smell, taste, and touch.

For this example, we will look at a retail space. It is a clothing shop that is in fashion and wants to continue getting publicity with the introduction of sensory design in its stores. A space within the store that is usually relatively utilitarian, the floor area, with the clothing racks, shelving, displays, and try-on rooms is a great chance to embellish the sensory program. The chosen senses are interestingly taste, as well as smell and touch. The other senses, vision and hearing, are already addressed with the actual clothing, advertising, and instore displays, as well as the music and verbiage of the employees in the store.

The problem with fashion is that it changes over time, so the experiential moments should be temporary, that is being present in the store from one month to one year, depending on the campaign and design intentions. So, these moments should be easy to change over the weeks of the marketing effort, but the inputs should be similar enough that a theme is clear and relevant.

First, we will look at using smell. Commonly, we will use a subtle, pervasive scent, but in this case, because of the client, it is likely appropriate to create a smell landscape with varying scents. Unlike, in other examples, these scents do not need to be subtle. Instead, they should be localized so there is variation across the store – little moments of scent that garnish the store experience. What is funny is smells go in and out of style, so it is required, to keep the store current, to use a scent expert or a designer that understands the fashion to choose the scents. Nevertheless, for this example we will choose acceptable smells for the time of this writing. First, we will use orange zest, which has the classic smell of orange, but provides a ping of citric that is very common in processed foods. It smells excellent and is easy to obtain. This scent can be on cards, in a liquid form, or raw in a small bowl as if they are to be used in cooking.

The next scent is a combination, like a chord of smells, relying on the low subtle smell of cucumber and the sharp points of cayenne. This is a soothing smell that occasionally spanks those experiencing it. There is a great deal of contrast in the parts, which makes it enticing. Although we could rely on only cayenne, we would not have the enticing cucumber to draw in the user.

The final scent is that of fresh paper and artificial raspberry. This smell is again a combination, however it is not a complete change from sweet to sour, instead both are relatively enjoyable, but the artificial raspberry is the highlight that rounds out a somewhat flat smell of paper. Although the fine paper is a nice smell, it may be considered monotone. This scent would be on the packaging materials at the point of sale.

For taste, we would like to introduce food items that are used to entertain and augment the smell program. This could be free snacks, appetizers, and drinks. But, they could also be candy, gum and other junkfood. For this example, I suggest using candy with fruity flavors. This could be a hard candy or gummy. This will provide the tang, but other food items should be used to sooth and attract the customer. Then again, two items that would work very well are ice cream and flavors of fizzy water. Both of these are enjoyed by most people, they provide taste, as well as smell.

For touch, we would like moments throughout the store to allow physical interaction. They should be distinct but should all tie into the design scheme. For this project, I suggest starting with something quirky: perhaps, we can use rough stone busts of figures in popular culture. These busts should be near table height to encourage touching and should not easily degrade, with all of the handling.

Another touch experience is the use of corduroy or corrugated material on the wall, offset by half a unit to provide continuity but without complete alignment. These walls should be very near the customer and within reach. This will encourage the user to run their hands on the wall as they traverse the space.

Finally, changing the floor surfaces between parts of the floor and room is useful for both adding textural variety but also to designate spatial uses. When doing this, the designer can determine the meaning of the surface qualities–what does it mean to be smooth? Ridged?

All of these possibilities should be used regularly or periodically throughout the campaign, and it is not necessary to proscribe the experiential moments in the store or group of stores.

Touch: Simple Touch

Free Nerve Ending

Touch is the physical contact of the body with an object or element, providing a response that triggers some reaction in the brain. This sense is local and does not allow the individual to receive or provide a tactile response over distance. There are several types of touch with different mechanisms to provide varying experiences of the sense, and each of these will be explored. As such, this section will be different from the sections on the other four classic senses, vision, hearing, taste, and smell, as well as those such as chemoreception and time. Most forms of touch are on the exterior of the body, especially the skin. However, our interiors also are able to sense touch in various forms, such as tension and pain.

We use touch to understand our spatial relation to the world, brushing against the surface of any object within the environment. Depending on the part of the body that is providing the tactile sense, there are different sensations that can be experienced, and through experience and innate understanding, we are able to differentiate the feelings and provide a response in reaction. Some forms of touch are pleasurable, but many are not, and the body must take any cues that are available to keep itself in a safe position. When used in relation to other senses, such as hearing or vision, we are able to use touch to understand the form and makeup of many or most objects, without requiring the dissection or definition of them. This intuition represents the powerful interplay of the sense of touch with the brain, where the body can provide sensory input, and the mind creates models or understanding.

Touch could be the first sense in our evolution. The receptors and the interaction with the brain can be said to be relatively simple in relation to the other senses, especially hearing and vision. We can argue touch is very close to taste, because the elements must come into contact with the body to ensure there is a reaction to the elements explored. Smell is similar in some ways because it uses a simple interaction with the environment to produce the sense response.

We must use touch when other senses are lacking, however the intimate connection that is provided with the sensation, because of proximity, makes it a sense that can act successfully alone or in combination with one or more of the other sensory modes. There may be a very immediate understanding of the world through the various forms of touch which are not possible with other senses, such as vision. This is because touch is immediate and present, whereas the other senses, besides taste, require some translation or definition of meaning in the brain for understanding. For one without experience with a new object, the nature and importance of the novel element is unknown, and it is necessary to learn what the object is, whether at distance or by contact. We can say this is the case with touch, however the interaction and instant sensing of the object in question make understanding extremely fast – as fast as the speed of electricity through the nervous system.

We use touch in times without other senses, but also in combination with other senses to have a complete experience of the object. This can take place at anytime and anywhere, and our bodies are constantly taking touch information that can be filtered out. Arguably, any form of touch can be turned off or hidden through the brain to avoid constant response to a persistent input. However, some might say that pain is not avoidable. This could very well be true, and it is extremely important for the body to be protected and without danger. There are conditions that don't allow a person to feel pain, and though this at first thought could be wonderful, in reality, it is very dangerous. To think that one can put an appendage into a flame or slice the skin with a knife, and the individual feels no pain, this is very scary and likely will not allow the person to stay healthy, as there are hazardous things everywhere in the world, and the body needs this sense of pain to avoid the dangerous.

The sense above is nociception, the sense of pain, but there are many for touch. Some of the other senses of touch are: pressure, itch, cold thermoception, heat thermoception, proprioception, tension, stretch, vibration, equilibrioception (which some might lump with hearing), thirst, and hunger. Each of these has specific mechanics and a special response in the brain. We will look at each of these separately, but for now, we will look at these all as the general sense of touch.

As mentioned before, touch is very personal and must occur at the object or person. This is the same with taste, and taste has various types which tell the mind and body what is being consumed. Similarly, touch has many types that provide different pieces of information to the brain. The other senses, vision, hearing, and smell, use distance and can provide a sense of spatial relationships and size. Whereas, touch has a limited ability to experience the magnitude of space, only able to measure with the count of sensors and movement across a surface. This can be useful when the other senses are limited, but it is not efficient and it requires the user to be in contact with the planes and edges of a space or object.

One might argue that many or most forms of touch are binary, only having an on and an off. However, with the introduction of multiple touch sensors and multiple types of those touch sensors, we develop a sense of magnitude as well as directionality. To do this, the touch sensors must be arranged in an array, and the sensors are wired together and coordinated at the brain to provide mapping of an environment. If there are limited touch sensors, the body must probe locations over time and rely on memory to produce a map of a space or object.

The sense of touch is so simple in many of its forms that the experience of sensing is only heightened through the lack of use. That is, if something is touched constantly, then there is no reaction and no meaning. However, if there is space or time between activating touch, the experience and meaning are heightened.

With this understanding of limiting the use of touch, it should be the designer's goal to use the sense strategically and only on occasion. To use it constantly would overwhelm the user and lessen the experience. But, when should someone use the sense? Because it is more effective with limited use, it is best to use touch at specific moments when it is necessary to grab the user's attention in conjunction with another sense, such as hearing or smell. You find people do this in daily conversation. Someone might touch another's arm to add gravity or focus to spoken words. The added sense heightens the intensity of an interaction to throw someone into a new understanding or experience. The worst time to use touch is when trying to show objectivity and to sway someone. Because the sense of touch is very intimate and up front, the use of the sense should be invited and desired by the subject. Otherwise, the use of the sense might be inappropriate or even abusive. For things that should be removed from immediate experience, the use of the senses that can be used across space are better. These senses are vision, hearing, and smell, which all can provide experience but they are less invasive and do not intrude on personal space as we interact with the physical environment.

Touch can be a very strong solution for design, because it is used by everyone and the sense experience can vary over time or by the user to create everchanging interactions. Whereas, other senses such as taste and smell can be argued to be limited to a set number of feelings, given by the number of receptors. Even vision and hearing may not have many variations, especially vision. Hearing allows variation by tone, depending on the source. However, touch can have variation that is private and personal, in that the touch is local and is not shared unless another is at the source of the sense experience. The other senses, besides taste, are shared among the individuals in the space, so they can be said to be public. Touch and taste can be said to be private.

We can use touch in multiple ways. First, we have tactile objects and forms that we touch. However, there is also the opposite where the object or surface touches the user. This is a nice solution for dynamic design, where the touch experience is in movement and addresses the user. A third type of touch is where objects or entities touch one another. This is somewhat foreign, but it allows us to be empathetic and virtually experience the sensation. However, one might argue this is the use of vision. Finally, there is the individual touching another living entity. Again, this is a very personal experience and can only occur with the permission of both parties.

Touch is a useful sense for design, because it is pervasive and immediate. We can use it for any and every design, and it would not seem out of place. The hands and body allow us to transfer knowledge without communicating with words. In addition, this transference can take place without the use of vision, which tends to be the sense we lean into most. As such, we can have sensory experience without looking, and we can have multiple inputs across the body to provide two or more meanings. However, it is usually better to provide a consistent message in a design, even with multiple inputs.

A change to make touch a central sense for design is the transformation of a space to allow repetitive or continuous interface with surfaces to allow the body to take the design intent. This would mean changing the dimensions and orientation of the spaces to provide a more constricted and folded space to ensure the body has access to surfaces as moments of experience. So, a great volume would not be best to provide a textural narrative, instead a space that is more like a corridor or well-furnished room will provide better opportunities to tell a story through touch. One of the best and most consistent surfaces for touch is the floor, which must always be traversed. The floor can have various materials and textures, but it must be clear for the designer what and when to use these textures, otherwise the meaning could be lost.

To improve the use of touch in design, we should have a thesis for our design. Then, the senses should be tools that are used specifically and aptly to tell the desired story. This would probably mean that we should be sparing in the sensory inputs to limit experiential overload, in most instances. With fewer experiences, it is easier to control the story, and the more sense inputs we add, the closer we should watch the meaning and definition of the sense.

If we were to only use touch, we should have a base state, and then have a clear intent with the material or texture added for variation. What are the meanings of various materials and textures? Are soft things happy and comfortable? Are hard and sharp things mean and standoffish? Are these understandings of materials common across cultures? Some surely are, as we experience these forms of touch with the body, and the body attempts to find a state of comfort and safety continuously. A rigid and ridged object will likely provide some form of excitement and not lull the user into sleep. However, surely there are variations in meanings of materials from person to person and culture to culture. Some might find the warm and fuzzy experience of flannel as comforting, while others might find it hot and overwhelming. In addition, the way the sense is experienced may agitate some but soothe others. For example, running your bare feet across a swath of carpet could be satisfying for you, but bother another, like fingernails on a blackboard.

It is hard to have a design that does not incorporate touch through at least the feet and floor. However, touch is not required for design, even though it tends to be present at least in the materiality of the design output. In this way, the designer should acknowledge the presence of the sense of touch and provide a clear use of the sense in at least the places where the human body comes into contact with the design installation. With this, we can look at various uses of touch. Touch can be used to provide a visceral reaction, convey information, complement meaning from another sense, and counter another sense.

To use touch, we require our body, and with the body in a space, we have presence. Therefore, touch requires and exploits presence. We cannot have a haptic or textural landscape at distance, so this can attract and ingratiate people to and in a space, especially in a world that relies so much on the digital and virtual. A website or social media surface cannot provide touch variations, and the designer can capitalize on this to bring people to a space or place that provides the sense. In contrast, we can remove the sense of touch to deprive and direct through the use of pauses in stimulation – a cold, hard space is not likely to make people linger. Furthermore, the hint of the lack of experience can push individuals to move to another space in a sensory form of propaganda, the bandwagon or the fear of missing out.

Beyond the simplest form of touch we will examine: Pressure, Itch, Cold Thermoception, Heat Thermoception, Proprioception, Tension, Stretch, Vibration, and Equilibrioception.

Simple Touch Precedents

Texture on handles and handlebars to signal end or transition.

Braille.

Smooth, polished surface for cleanliness or luxury.

Clothing fabric interaction while moving.

Palimpsest of that before.

Floor surface at entries and curb cuts.

Tool texture showing how and where to hold it.

Wall surface changes based on use and location (offices and hospitality).

Speed bumps and strips on roadways.

Surface relief variation on drawing / writing surface (rubbings).

Simple Touch Possibilities

Convey information on handles, rails, furniture, or devices (objects touching body).

Map another sense when unable to use other sense because of environment or disability.

Affect emotions and enrich environment.

Diversion, Entertainment, and Variation.

Reminder (future) or Memorial (past) of action, event, person or thing.

Warning of hazard or boundary.

Instructions or Directions.

Mapping or Wayfinding.

Encourage specific behavior, such as slowing down, silence, turning.

Alter or augment items and motions by superimposition.

Simple Touch Sensors

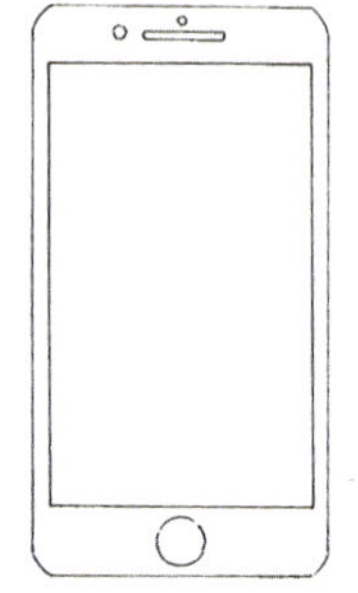

Capacitance Sensor

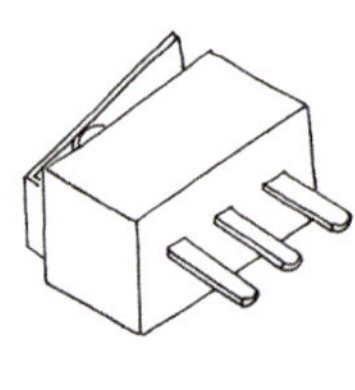

Contact Switch

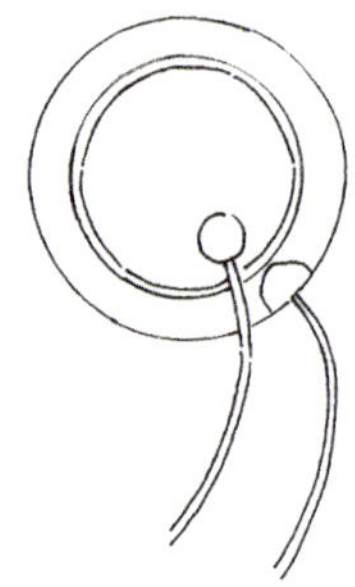

Piezo Element

Simple Touch Actuators

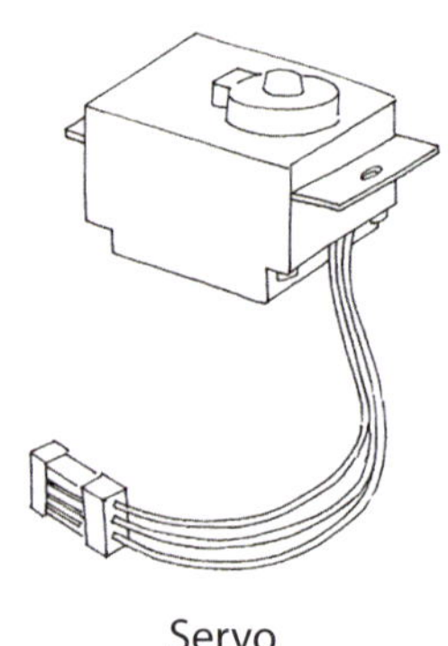

Servo

Simple Touch Interpretations

sharp
angular
rough
crevices
projections

angry

cleaved curvilinearity
asymmetry
beyond human scale
surprising roughness
hollows

anxious

regularly ridged
slight chamfer on transitions
singular directionality
tapering
cool

confident

angular geometry
rough texture
linear
orthogonal patterning
strenuous to move

determined

inviting smoothness
rounded
moments of delightful variation
convex
warm

happy

flat
filleted edges
large depressions
regularly patterned
velvety

meditative

wispy
changing with movement
limp
network of linear elements
warm

perplexed

extremely smooth
hollow tube
singular, rounded projection
dull edges
rubbery

withdrawn

Touch: Pressure

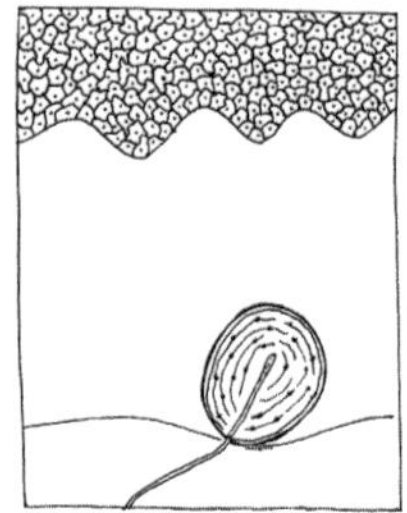

Pacinian Corpuscle

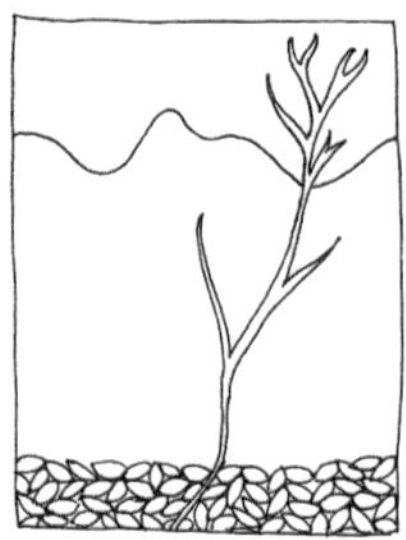

Free Nerve Ending

The Pacinian corpuscle and free nerve endings are used to sense pressure. Besides pressure, this corpuscle also senses vibrations. Pacinian corpuscles are located deeper in the skin than another touch sensor, the Meissner corpuscle, which we will discuss later, and the Pacinian corpuscles contain specialized sensory cells that respond to pressure and mechanical stimulation. When something presses the skin, it affects the Pacinian corpuscle, and this sends signals to the brain. The brain processes the stimuli, and we perceive these as a sensation of pressure.

Free nerve endings are found in the skin and are responsible for detecting pressure, pain, temperature, and other sensations. These nerve endings are not associated with any specialized sensory cells, and are instead found throughout the skin, including the deeper layers. When something applies pressure to the skin, it stimulates the free nerve endings, which in turn send a signal to the brain, which it processes, and we perceive the signal as a sensation of pressure.

Using pressure is not very common in architecture and design. There are physical phenomena that change the pressure of a space, such as weather, elevation, and depth, however designers usually look past this form of touch. Nonetheless, an architect can use the sense by affecting the size and shape of spaces – in order to use pressure, we must add either density to the air or pressure to the body. Both will work, but it is much easier to apply pressure through materials, actuators, and physical interaction. The question is what is the meaning behind the introduction of pressure – is it warm and welcoming like an embrace, or is it overbearing and dangerous, like a crushing weight? Furthermore, are there other meanings to the sense? We can apply some through storytelling. Narrative can run along cultural lines, or it can expand beyond, into new realms. However, we must have a reason for the introduction of the sense, to ensure that it is not frivolous and gimmicky.

The first thing to improve pressure in design is to acknowledge its necessity and use. This can be done with the introduction of a compressing aperture, like a narrow doorway with elasticity. This first experience places it in the menu of possible interactions within a space. Then, we must understand the story that is being told by the designer, and use pressure sparingly to provide an experiential moment. Minimal use is important, especially at first. If desired, the design can build to a climax where the user is placed under pressure, which could be either a calming effect or a choking effect, depending on application. The designer must take great care to guide the user to one of these places, or another, as poorly communicated intentions can create adverse effects. Instead, try to have a simple story and simple plot, expressed through the senses.

If design were only pressure, then it would be quite surreal, but possibly a harkening back to the womb. Most of us do not remember this experience, but a part of our brain may have a reaction to such a sensation. However, pressure does not only need to provide safety or comfort, but it also can communicate meaning. Think about how someone who cares for another will squeeze a shoulder or press their torso to another's as a hug. These show caring, but what about someone who shakes hands too hard? Is this done to show caring? No, not likely. Instead, it is meant to show strength and some form of superiority, whether true or not. So, as stated earlier, the designer must have a strong understanding of the introduction of pressure, and also know what it means.

If design doesn't incorporate pressure, that is not necessarily a bad thing, but it is an important type of touch that can be employed relatively easily. Most design does not include actual pressure. In fact, a lot of design doesn't have to, with so many senses to explore. But, it is immediate and personal and, although design does not need to include it, pressure is a relatively simple way to convey belonging or caring.

Some alternative uses for pressure include mapping or translating information from one sensory output to another. Also, sound is really air pressure, so the sense of pressure can mimic the effects of sound. In use, pressure can rise and fall, providing a meaning. Furthermore, a story arc can be represented by the shape of the curve, and the ups and downs of the curve can be expressed by rising and lowering pressure.

Adapting pressure to an existing structure can be difficult, unless walkways, corridors, and spaces are robust enough to meet the codes while interacting with the user through pressure. However, the introduction of the sense in places of movement or personal spaces are definitely possible. Movement is able to provide the input of pressure through acceleration. Personal spaces allow pressure to be applied like or by clothing, and doing such can be rather simple for placing pressure on the user consistently, but the variation of the sense and novel application can create new experiential moments that change the individual.

To use pressure, we should start with no pressure, then we would build up the sense and its placement. We must remember that pressure is on a continuous spectrum, where the introduction of pressure is not just on and off again, like 0s and 1s. Instead, it builds fractionally or steadily, and it is not just yes or no, but partially, like baby steps to experience. This can create more nuance for a structure, not just knocking the patron over the head with information.

Pressure Precedents

Medical equipment that directs the posture and position of the body (bed, braces, limb supports, bandaging).

Individuals directing movement; pushing an individual.

Embrace, hugging, or physical touching.

Compressive clothing for athletic use.

Compressive clothing for autism and sensory issues.

Adjustable chairs and furniture cushioning.

Massage and /or masseuse.

Positive and Negative air pressure for conditioned and protected spaces (hospitals and labs).

Funnels and dies.

Pressure cooker to decrease cooking time.

Pressure Possibilities

Indicate the location of another person or object.

Urge individual in a certain direction.

Express physical touch or embrace over distance.

Translate information from other sense.

Direct use of specific body parts, such as fingers, arms, or legs.

Monitor another's vital signs.

Relieve muscle soreness and mental stress (massage).

Counter or enhance environmental pressure, such as under water or in space.

Reshape objects for specific use.

Increase physical performance.

Pressure Sensors

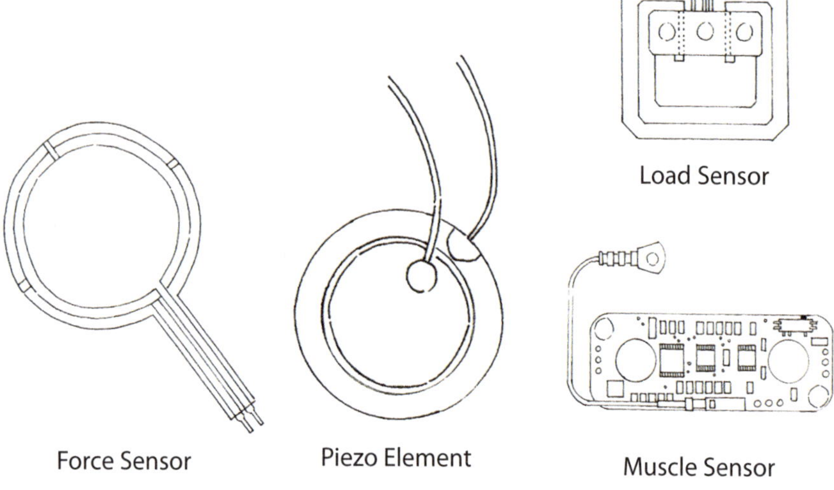

Pressure Actuators

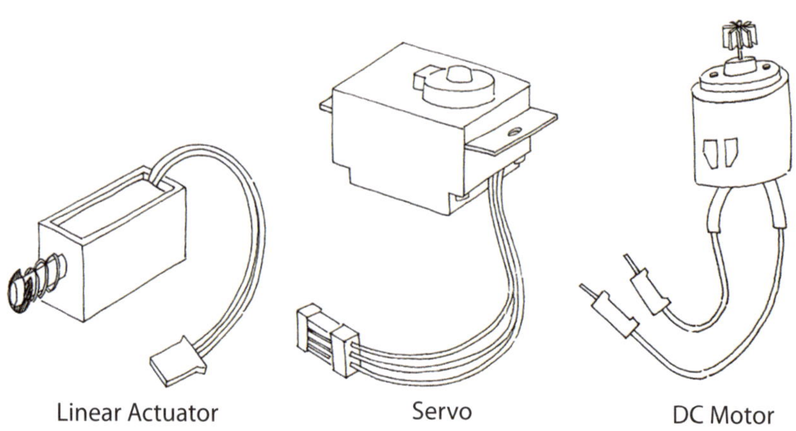

Pressure Interpretations

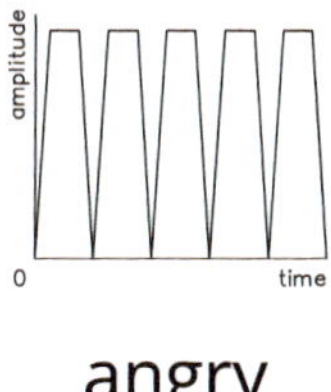

angry

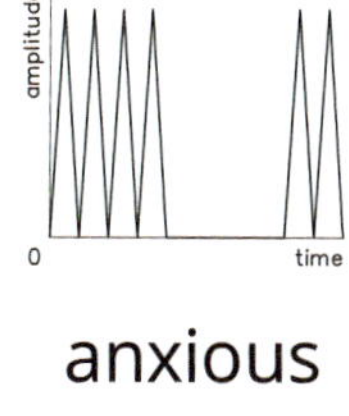

anxious

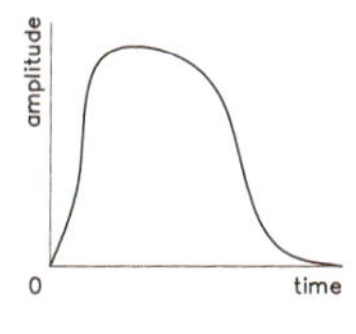

confident

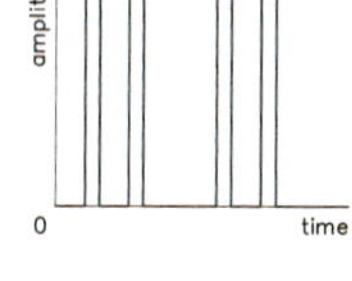

determined

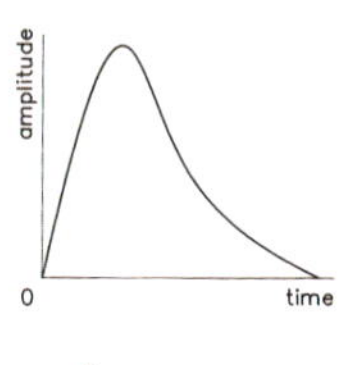

happy

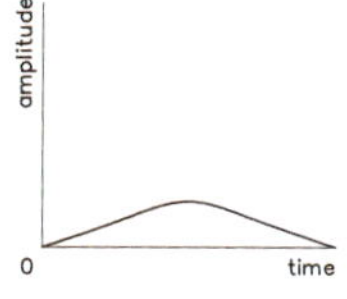

meditative

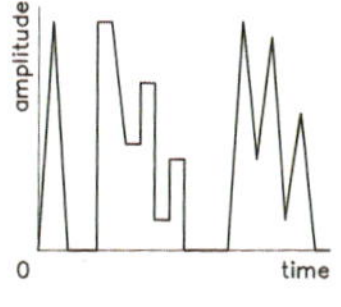

perplexed

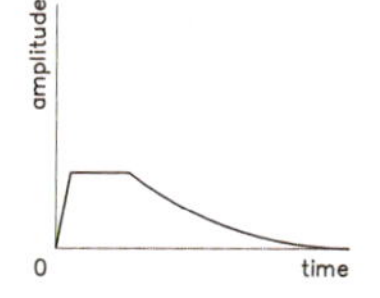

withdrawn

Touch: Itch

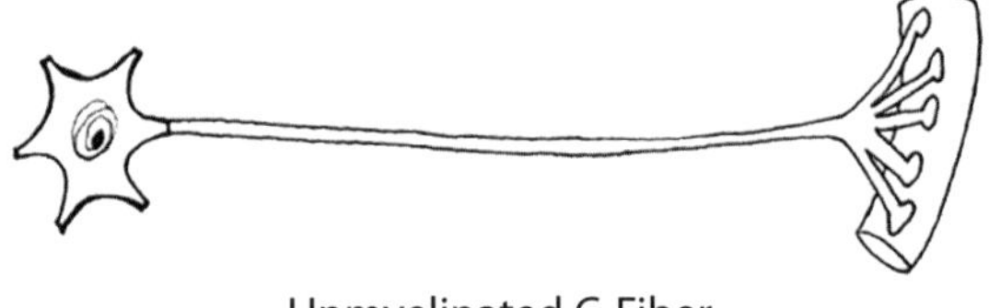

Unmyelinated C-Fiber

Unmyelinated C-fibers are a nerve fiber found in the skin that provide the sensation of itch. These fibers are not coated with a protective layer of myelin, like other forms of nerve fibers. The lack of myelin allows these fibers to transmit sensations more quickly than other types. If something irritates the skin and causes an itch, it stimulates the unmyelinated C-fibers, which send a signal to the brain. The brain processes this signal, providing the perception of itch.

Using the unmylienated fibers to induce itch is a questionable but potent way to create a sensation in the user. The problem with the use of the sense is how to ensure the itch is desired and is not overwhelming to those that experience it. Is itch a positive experience? In very moderate amounts, itch can be acceptable and maybe even pleasurable. By activating the sense, we can use it to provide a warning in cases where a silent but intense signal is necessary. This would be a more amplified signal to ensure the user senses the signal. Again, in most applications, we will want a weak to moderate activation of the sense of itch.

Most design does not accommodate itch as a sense, and it is usually avoided. However, to create a rounder, more full sensory experience, it is a possible tool to include in the design and the design's development. In very small amounts, itch can be ignored or blocked out, however as it grows, the sense of itch can feel interminable. Although it is not pain, itch will give negative feelings and associations with overuse. So, subtle stimulation of the sense through a mist, temperature change, or application of a chemical can provide more than enough of the sensory experience. Furthermore, it will be necessary to provide a chemical or treatment to remove the sense – we do not want a design experience to be like getting poison ivy or chicken pox – we want it to be an instant experience that wears off very quickly to avoid irritating the user. This may be through the interface with a chemical applied to a paper, textile surface, or the skin, then a second chemical application subdues the experience. This needs to be resolved through the design process, through trial and error.

For better or worse, itch is never the sole sense that is provided in a design. If it were the only input, then the user would have a very monochromatic experience that relied on the lack or presence of itch in various amounts. The variation on the itch sense is limited, so the ebb and flow of the experience would need to be provided through activating an array of the fibers to produce the desired effect. A single location will create a near binary experience of itch or non-itch.

Most forms of design do not include the experience of itch, so it is not surprising to have a design without it. Instead, we should think about the absence of itch, which will provide a sense of relief in many, but it might also deaden the experience for the user if it is wholly ignored throughout a project or environment. In nature, the activation of this sense is a warning to avoid something.

With the activation of many itch locations on the body, we can provide levels of the experience, but also directionality. The increasing levels of itch can be mapped and correlate with some input in the world or in society. If we want to keep attention on an event or on indices, this will up the ante on the user's acceptance and judgement on the use of the sense. A very great itch could signal worse outcomes for the stock market. This is an indirect relationship, but we can also use a direct relationship, say in virtual reality with the representation of insects or a wool sweater your grandmother gave to you. We are able to make the experience move around the body which will create a rounder experience. This can be used with other forms of touch, as well. Say we want to pull the user around, can we create an itch sensation on their back and then turn that experience off after the body has rotated? How would we do this? Through actuators or chemical interaction?

Adapting itch to an existing structure is complicated and possibly difficult. Although we have access to ways to activate, it might be better to look away from the building and focus on the elements that come into contact with the skin. These include wall surfaces and fixtures, but also should include clothing and furniture. We are not likely to touch the ceiling or roll on the floor, but we can be expected to sit in a chair or place our hands on a table while talking or reading.

Designing for itch will include variations of the amount of the stimulant, but it should also be about the absence of the sense. The designer must keep in mind that not everyone will want to experience this sense nor will they feel the effects without a high enough amplitude of the sense.

Itch Precedents

Poison ivy and oak.

Allergies.

Caustic materials, substances.

Phantom itch: presence of absence.

Irritating fabrics or surfaces (wool, fur).

Small animals and insects.

Reaction to medications.

Shedding elements, such as skin and hair.

Illnesses of skin and other parts.

Nerve damage.

Itch Possibilities

Call attention to body part or clothing that needs attention.

Alarm for event that occurs or will occur.

Your direct body part two of position or direction.

Warning against danger.

Divert attention from pain or the unpleasant.

Provide slight discomfort to improve performance.

Color or affect information from other senses to alter meaning.

Deter use of object or element.

Use in combination with other senses for entertainment.

Improve and encourage physical behavior.

Itch Sensors

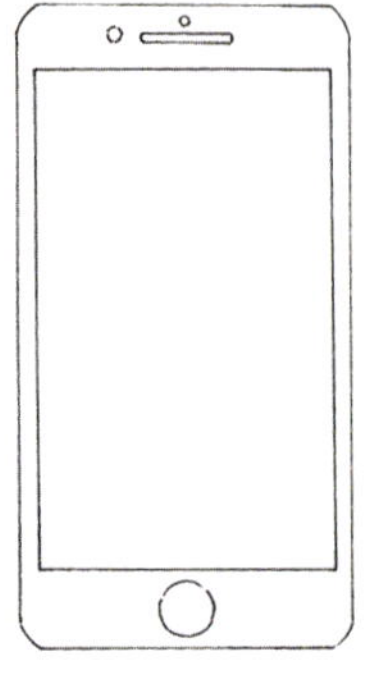

Capacitance Sensor

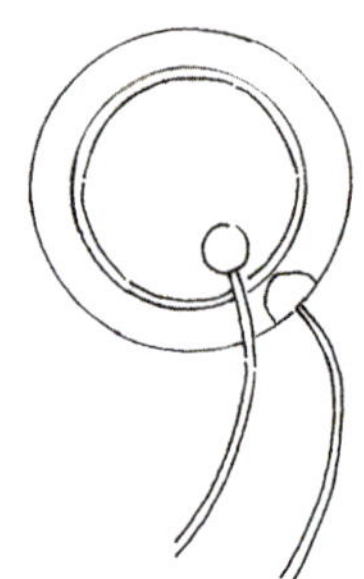

Piezo Element

Itch Actuators

Wool and Itchy Materials

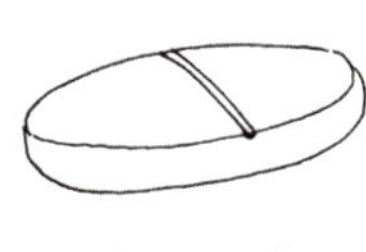

Chemicals

Natural Irritants

Itch Interpretations

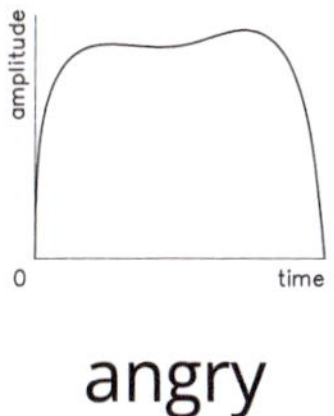

angry

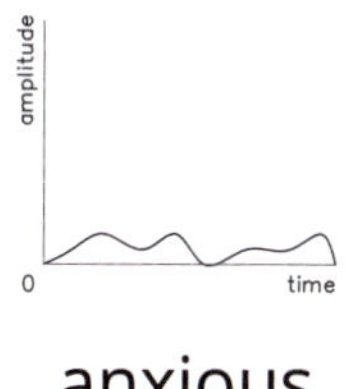

anxious

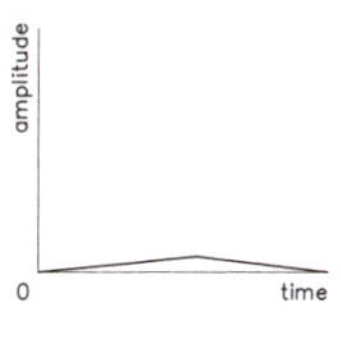

confident

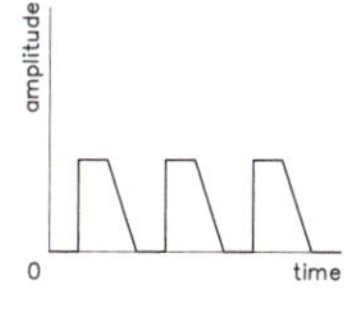

determined

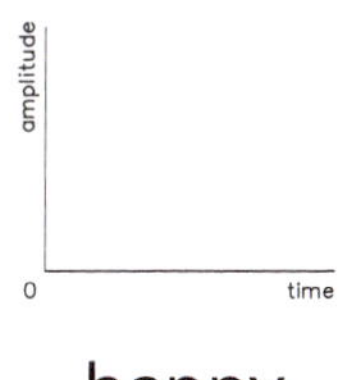

happy

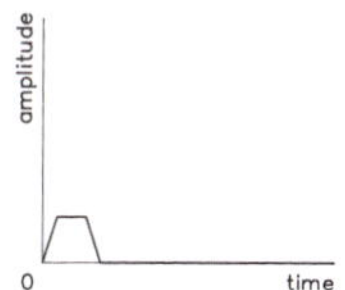

meditative

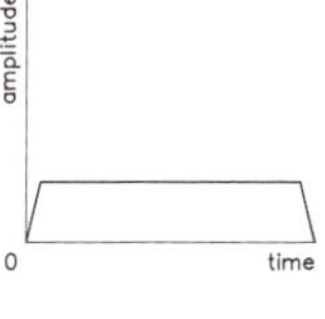

perplexed

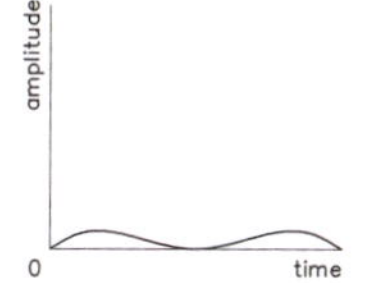

withdrawn

Touch: Cold Thermoception

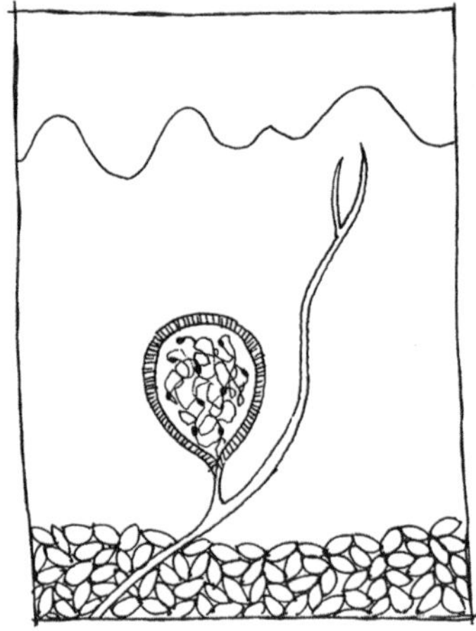

Krause End Bulb

The Krause end bulb is a nerve ending found in the skin that detects changes in temperature, especially cold temperature. These nerve endings contain specialized sensors that are sensitive to changes in coolness, and when something cold comes into contact with the skin, it stimulates this Krause end bulb. In turn, the end bulb sends a signal to the brain, and the brain processes this information, resulting in our perception of the sensation of cold.

The use of temperature, especially cold thermoception requires us to change temperatures from a baseline to allow variation in experience. The baseline would be a tepid temperature, which would vary with the ambient temperature, as the seasons provide differences that our bodies accommodate, so a lukewarm temperature in summer will be warmer than the lukewarm temperature in winter. In any case, our bodies thrive with change, and the best cold experience will be that which contrasts with the hot or tepid. In addition, we do not want to have consistently low temperatures, which would nullify the effect of cold experience. With this said, we must have full control of the space where we incorporate cold thermoception into the design, which means a permanent space is likely to be interior, although we can have a temporary design installation in the late-spring, summer, and early-fall seasons that highlights cold.

Before using cold thermoception, the designer should understand the meaning of the experience of cold. Of course, a breeze of cold air on a hot day is pleasurable, but is there another meaning to cold? Some would say that the cold is about death and nothingness, while other cultures might feel that the cold brings creation of form, making the abstract or nebulous concrete. In most instances, architects and designers only think about temperature in relation to comfort, but cold, just like the other senses can convey information and encourage certain feelings or thoughts. We must ensure that we understand the context we are bringing the cold sensation to and then have a distinct and specific meaning for the application of the temperature difference. When using cold thermoception, it is most likely that the designer will also want to include heat thermoception, which, though using different sensors, provides similar experiential qualities with the undulation in temperatures.

If one were only to use cold thermoception in a design, the experience would be limited in dimension, as well as use of the senses. Our body is able to experience cold through sensors in the skin, but to feel a great difference in cold, other than a minor change to ambient temperatures, we must allow time for the cold to sink in to provide an understanding of the magnitude of cold. This is not viable in many instances, as we must control the entire environment's temperature, and we may not want to put the user through such extremes, which could cause sickness or possibly even death. Nevertheless, to use only cold thermoception, we must have a higher temperature to provide a differential which allows the experience of cold.

Beyond the temperature of a conditioned space, most design does not incorporate cold thermoception, so it is an opportunity to explore what the sense can provide to the visitor. Without the cold, we have a continuous moderate to warm temperature which could feel dull and monotonous. This might be the intention of the designer, and so it is a point that no variation will provide a very static environment. As such, other senses may need to be toned down to complement the effect, or the designer may want variation to contrast the cold thermoception sensory experience.

Again, the use of cold thermoception requires variation of temperatures to feel the full import of the change to cold. Without this actual and experienced change, we would not register the cold temperature. With this variation in temperature, there should be some meaning that is associated with the coolness, and this is based on the cultural context. What is the cultural meaning for cold in the location of the design? When working with cold, first design with the tepid and the hot – this will allow the experience to fully develop.

In an existing space, we must control the temperature for a baseline, then introduce the cold inputs. Will this be with blowing air? Refrigerated surfaces? Ice with food and drinks? It is very likely that the use of cold thermoception will work in conjunction with other senses to create the sensory moment. As such, it is important for the designer to have full control of the narrative that is desired, so that the interaction of the various senses does not create a muddled experience because of interference. Furthermore, the designer must not intend to use cold thermoception constantly, so that the experience of cold is registered by the user.

To counter the experience of cold, we can of course use heat, however what other senses or emotions can we use? With concentration or ire, the visitor can overcome or ignore the feeling of cold. Furthermore, with separation, the user does not need to experience cold thermoception, as it can be removed from touch and insulated.

Cold Thermoception Precedents

Air-conditioning for space.

Compress for injury / soreness.

Cold water for overheated body.

Cold neck towel to lower apparent temperature.

Burns and other wounds.

Then for airflow to lower temperature.

Refrigeration for food.

Cooling to promote airflow.

Lower humidity and collect condensation.

Increase electronics efficiency.

Cold Thermoception Possibilities

Counter environmental conditions.

Indicate status of parts or elements.

Heighten alertness.

Raise energy level in space.

Cool body in high activity.

Provide discomfort to limit behavior.

Increase comfort in sleep.

Lower pain in body when applied.

Map other senses and information.

Indicate services are not accessible or off-limits.

Cold Thermoception Sensors

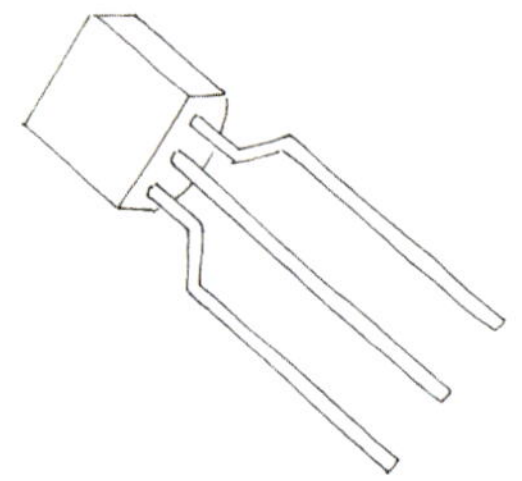

Temperature Sensor

Cold Thermoception Actuators

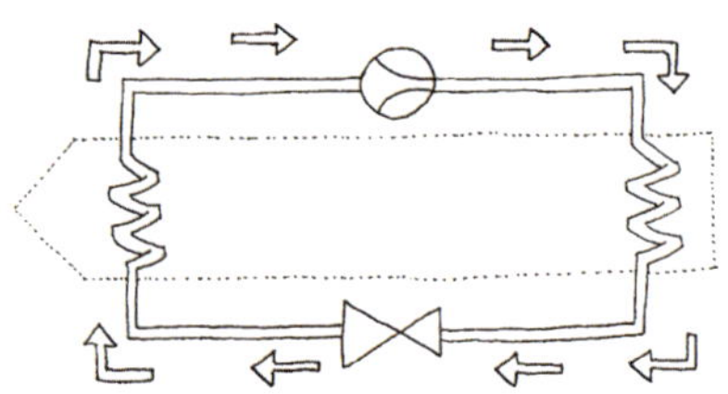

Cooling System

Cold Thermoception Interpretations

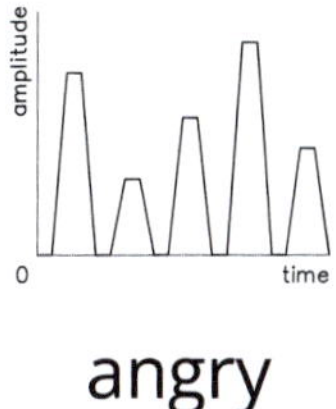

angry

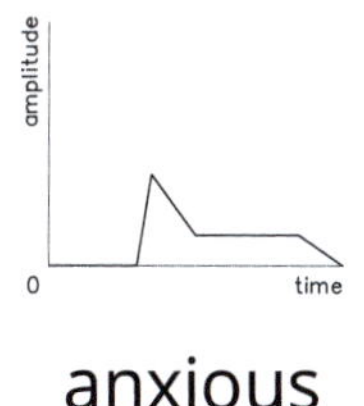

anxious

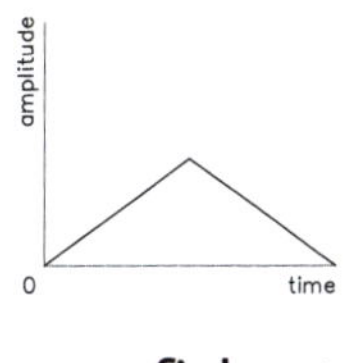

confident

determined

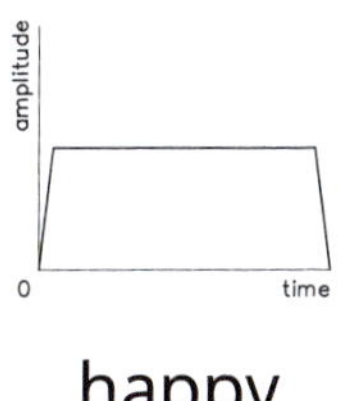

happy

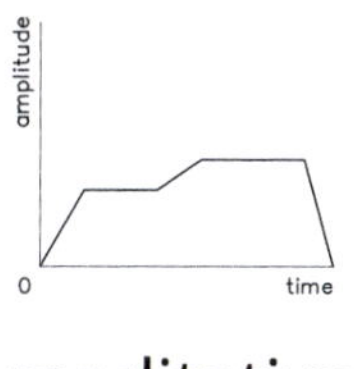

meditative

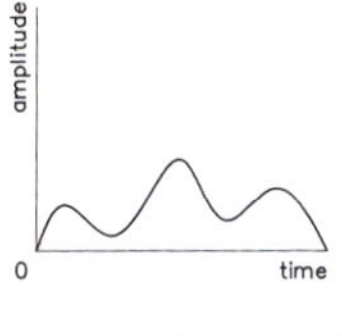

perplexed

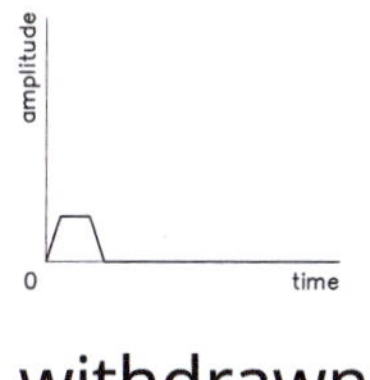

withdrawn

Touch: Heat Thermoception

Group C Nerve Fiber

The sense of heat is provided by Group C nerve fibers found in the skin. These fibers are sensitive to changes in temperature, and they respond to both warm and hot stimuli. When something with heat comes into contact with the skin, it stimulates the Group C nerve fibers, sending signals to the brain to process, which we perceive as a sensation of heat.

Although the physiological mechanics are different, heat thermoception goes together with cold thermoception, and like with cold thermoception, sensing heat requires a baseline that we can use to experience the differential in temperature. This baseline can be the ambient or tepid temperature, or for more dramatic effect, we can use colder temperatures to have a wider swing. This is interesting, because we can move between three regions of temperature, creating at least six different relationships. What does going hot to cold mean versus cold to hot? How does tepid to hot or hot to tepid compare to cold to hot or hot to cold? How about the effects of swinging temperatures between these ranges? Can we tell a story with just these?

To use heat thermoception, we must understand what the meaning of this sense brings. Heat will bring warmth and comfort, but it can also bring burning and pain. Furthermore, are there some groups that disdain warmth, or can they only thrive within it? What does warmth or heat symbolize culturally? This, as with most of the other senses, must be understood and used by the designer, because without this, the impact of the design would be lessened or lacking.

Like with cold thermoception, heat thermoception requires we incorporate heat intermittently for the user to acknowledge the presence and use the sense. Otherwise, the user will sit within the heat, not fully experiencing it and the knowledge or code being transmitted by the designer will not be taken or comprehended. Of course, the sense will be acknowledged if the designer has taken the time to create a meaning beyond the use of the sense, and it is evident that not working through the full extent of meaning will result in a design that is lackluster. Therefore, the designer should have this narrative spelled out, like a story card, through the drawings and models of the project.

If a design were only composed of heat thermoception, there would be a very narrow array of information that could be conveyed through the sense. Although we can sense heat, we have a limited range that we can feel it, meaning that the use of the sense is more or less off or on, and the way we understand how much greater the heat is, is through secondary effects on the body, such as sweat, overheating, and exhaustion. Without these other results, we are not able to produce a variation on the effects of heat, other than through the simple stimulation of the area where heat is sensed.

Other than controlling the ambient temperature, heat thermoception is typically ignored or avoided. Again, it is important to have a cultural understanding and knowledge of the context, and this is how the designer is able to organize and manage the narrative. Without the sense of heat, it is possible and most likely preferred for some designers that the sense is ignored. However, we must remember that it is another arrow in our quiver that allows us to tell a story and create interesting designs.

We can use heat to map on our bodies and in a space the locations of events and with the difference in temperature. In this way, we have a variable to provide a story. In other options, we can encourage the interaction of people with the use of heat and heat sensing. This is interesting, because we can use heat at a distance for some communication, but by touch for very specific needs. The question is how do we define the language and grammar with limited variables. Time and area are useful and of course the use of temperature variation helps. However, it might be simply a binary language or something akin to Morse code that we use. Again, is there any inherent meaning or symbolism present for the incorporation of heat into the design? Is it possible to create new meaning and symbolism?

We can retrofit an existing structure to incorporate heat by ensuring the temperature of the space is constant, and we can provide moments throughout the space that use heat thermoception. This cannot be continuous, or the variation and transmittance of information will not be observable. As mentioned above, we need to have differentiation in temperature over time, as well as through space. This change in temperature can be synced with other senses to create a sensory program. Can heat be used with smell to provide kind and friendly feelings? Can heat thermoception be used with pressure to create great intensity? How about using heat with sound to create off-balance designs for some purpose, such as psychedelia or evoking strong emotions?

Heat Thermoception Precedents

Heating for space.

Compress for injury / soreness.

Hot food and drink for cold bodies.

Heat pads for extremities. New healing burns and other wounds.

Fire to warm and welcome.

Stove, oven, etc. to heat food.

Heating to promote airflow.

Lower humidity and remove moisture.

Expand air for buoyancy.

Heat Thermoception Possibilities

Counter environmental conditions.

Indicate status of parts or elements.

Calm and soothe.

Lower energy; Heighten lethargy.

Encourage anger and discomfort.

Welcome and encourage user.

Lower pain in body when applied.

Map other senses' information.

Indicate surfaces are accessible or welcoming.

Allow body to proceed warm and cold environment.

Heat Thermoception Sensors

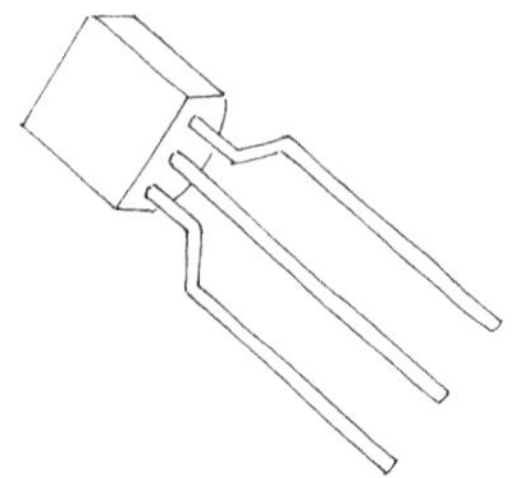

Temperature Sensor

Heat Thermoception Actuators

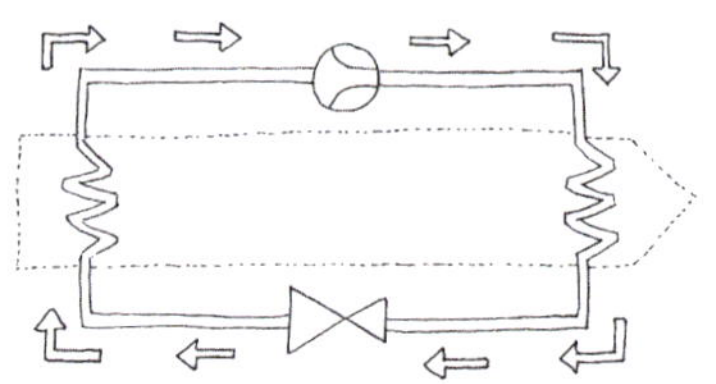

Heating System

Heat Thermoception Interpretations

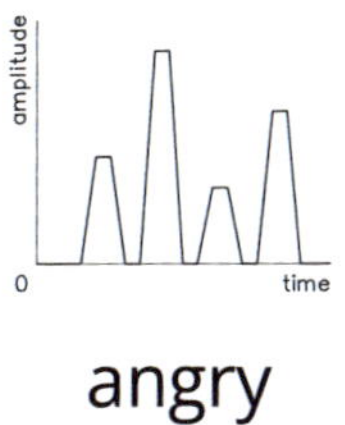

angry

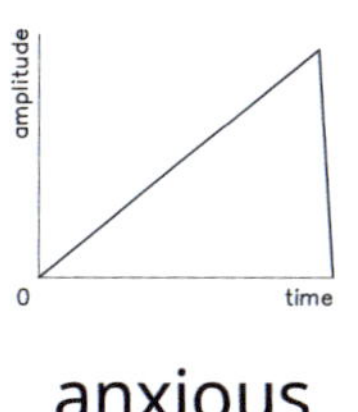

anxious

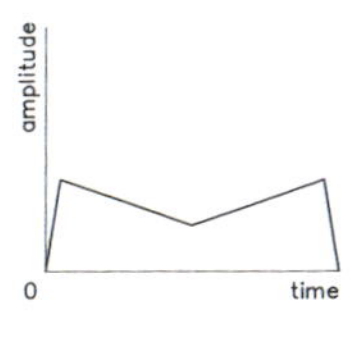

confident

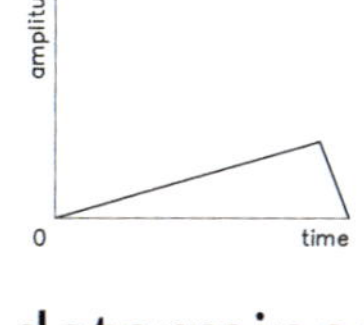

determined

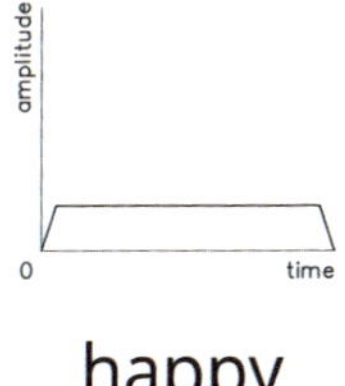

happy

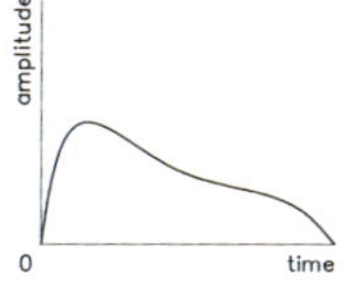

meditative

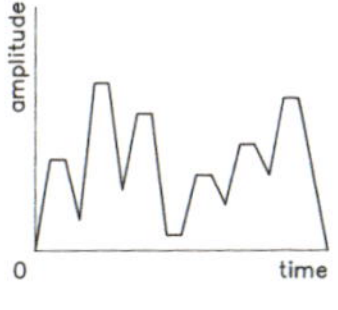

perplexed

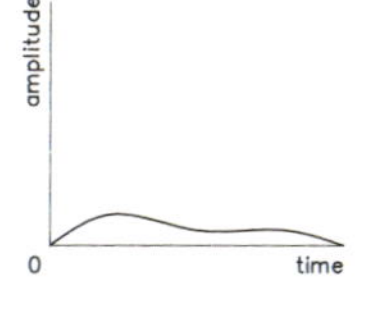

withdrawn

Touch: Proprioception

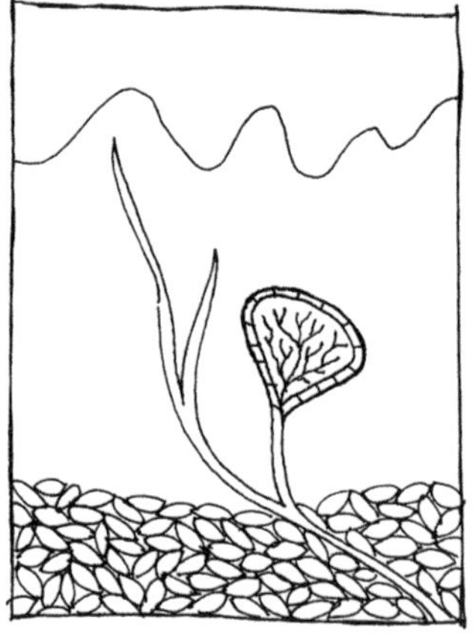

Ruffini Corpuscle

The sense of proprioception uses various sensors, including the Ruffini corpuscle. This Ruffini corpuscle is a type of nerve ending found in the skin that is responsible for detecting the stretching of the skin. These nerve endings are deep within the skin, and they hold specialized sensory cells that respond to mechanical stimulation. When something stretches the skin, this activates the Ruffini corpuscle, and it sends a signal to the brain, which processes the information, and we perceive it as a sensation of movement or position. This is proprioception: the sense of our body's position and movement.

Proprioception allows us to sense where our body is by determining position and orientation of our muscles. This is one of the most important senses to navigate through the world, because it governs our motions and movement through spaces. In order to use proprioception as a design tool, we must encourage or even force the user to move and articulate the body to express position and existence within a space. What is interesting about this sense is that it is internal and self referencing – most other senses require an external stimulus, but proprioception is all about the individual proceeding through space, guided by inherent senses. In addition, the same stimulus cannot be shared in a space without the conscious use of mimicry.

To use proprioception in design, we could force the body to use alternative postures and movement. Architecture today is more about inclusivity, where all spaces are traversable and everyone can use the space. This is very good for the rights of the people, but it doesn't promote individuals to explore the rotation and motion of the body through built work. As such, the space should not be exclusive, but it should allow anyone to try new orientations and positions of the body. Can we help people with their mobility and balance by introducing physical challenges in the space? A slope to the floor? A curvilinear space? A shelf that forces you to reach out?

If a design is only proprioception, then the installation is completely about the self, without any interaction with others. In theory, all of the users can exist within a space without having any need to touch or work together. By making the design about proprioception, the architect will have full control placed on the user and the design would work inside the user. This is intriguing and not typical for most other senses. Only equilibrium and the internal senses such as hunger and time are so singular and personal. The difference is that proprioception is about the action and position of the body, which is impressive and almost magical to have been evolved – if we had no proprioception, we would get hit by things, run over items, and very likely encounter obstructions or fall.

Because architectural design usually incorporates proprioception to some extent, to not include it in an installation would seem strange or odd. Proprioception can carry the design intentions very far, because it creates a dynamic, physical reaction which can enthrall the visitor rather than a passive, low energy sense that simply comes into our presence and then goes away. If it is the intention of the designer to create an installation that can be experienced from afar or with minimal effort, then it makes sense not to include proprioception. However, if the intention is to get the user moving, proprioception is one of the best senses to use when designing a space or structure.

Can we tell a story with proprioception? Can we make the use of the sense provide the ups and downs of a plot or narrative? What does it mean to the public but also to the individual? Is there a way to make the experience of the sense the same for everyone, or are we stuck with the individual interpretation? There must be some meanings that relate to the human form, especially those of body language. Can we make the user change to classic body positions to evoke or infuse certain feelings, such as having your head down could mean you are sad. What if we used the body language of emotions and told a narrative through that?

To use proprioception in an existing space, of course we will need to allow everyone to have access to the space. However, we can encourage the individual to be more adventurous and try new ways of inhabiting a space through orientation, position, and movement. If we left what was required in a space and then used the margins of this for exploring proprioception, this would be a very successful retrofit of a space. Furthermore, through physical and graphic encouragement, you can allow the individual to act out a play or story alone through position and movement.

Proprioception is the sense that promotes the individual to exist and subsist in a space without the need for other objects or people. Although, we do not want people to be completely introverted, to know yourself and be willing to learn more about the physical body and movement through space could very likely make individuals mentally healthier, if not just physically healthier. There have not been many that have explored this fully in design.

Proprioception Precedents

Proximity to people when talking.

Sports and athletic activities.

Embrace.

Spatial navigation, dimensions.

Furniture, such as sofa, chair, and bed.

Movement over terrain or within structures.

Balance and standing.

Hiding, fitting into spaces.

Envisioning body in another location or position.

Natural and developed reactions.

Proprioception Possibilities

Guide body through space.

Indicate proximity to objects and hazards.

Calm and placate.

Anger and barb.

Reminder or memorial.

Translate and map other senses, such as vision and sound.

Impede the use of an object or space.

Divert attention.

Indicate status of event or other entity.

Focus mind on certain ideas, elements, or spaces.

Proprioception Sensors

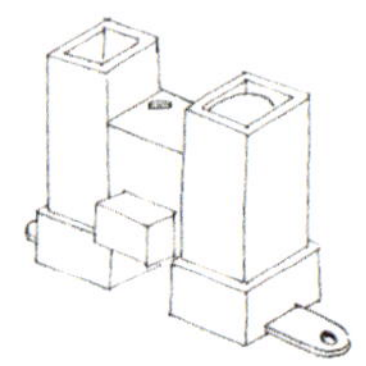

Infrared Rangefinder

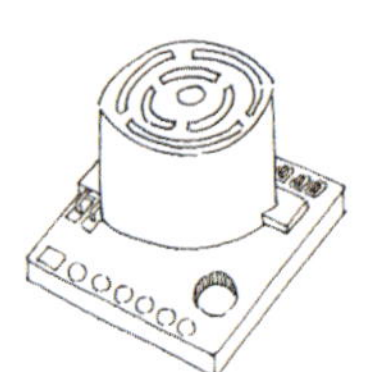

Sonic Rangefinder

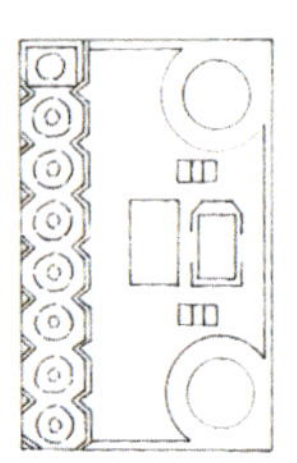

Accelerometer

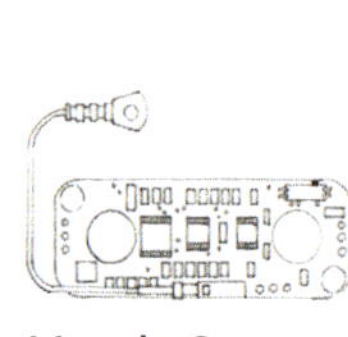

Muscle Sensor

Proprioception Actuators

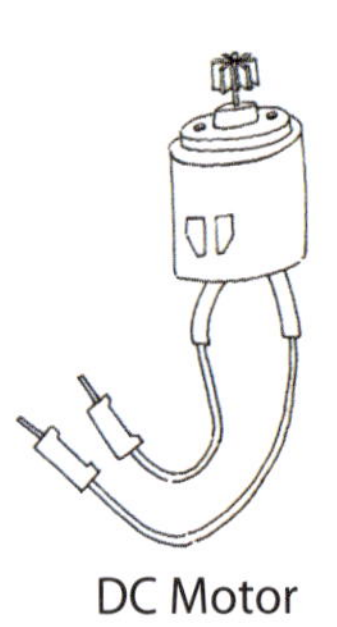

DC Motor

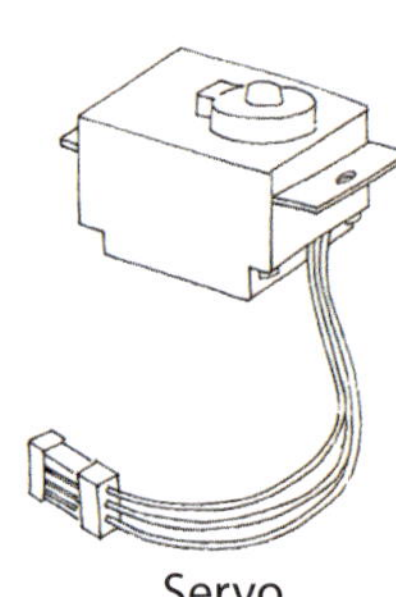

Servo

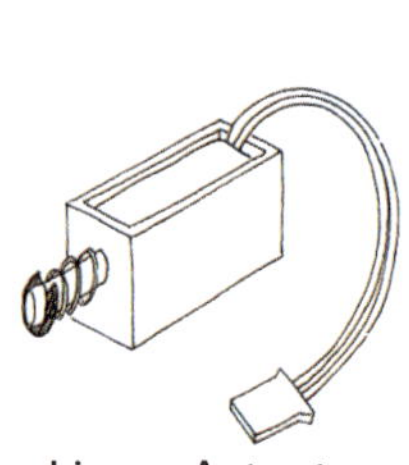

Linear Actuator

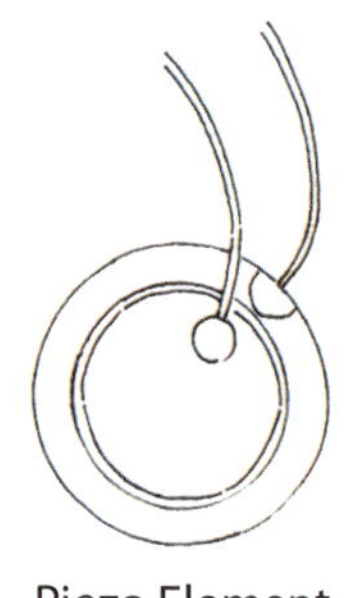

Piezo Element

Proprioception Interpretations

cramped long hallway
undulating ceiling near head
angular directional changes
floor elevation variation
occasional wall protrusions

angry

varying widths of space
changing tile floor surface
low continuous ceiling
brief open air moments
surprising cavities

anxious

slight incline
terraced
walls along one side
high, floating roof
directional

confident

tapering, narrowing corridor
descending
regularly placed wall planes
floor planks guide like rails
sublime, vaulting roof

determined

continuous slope
unimpeded
subtle surface changes
bound by low walls or trees
rhythmic enclosure change

happy

continuous direction
linear depression for path
level aggregate floor
cadence of walls lining
colossal structure

meditative

mazelike
multi-leveled
narrow passages
varying floor surfaces
monolithic band at headheight

perplexed

continuous floor plane
occasional impediments
continuous, low ceiling
sporadic elevation changes
walls implied by floor surface

withdrawn

Touch: Tension

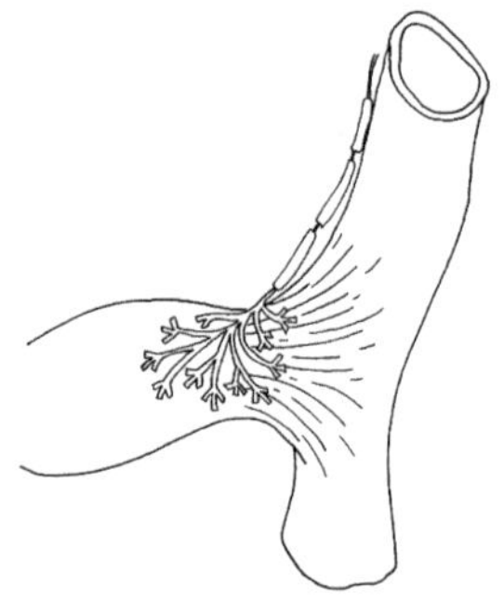

Golgi Tendon Organ Sensor

Golgi tendon organs are nerve endings found in tendons. These are part of fibrous connective tissue that attaches the muscles to bone. The Golgi tendon organ detects changes in tension in the tendon. These nerve endings contain specialized sensory cells that are sensitive to mechanical stimuli. When tension is applied to a tendon, the Golgi tendon organ is stimulated, which sends a signal to the brain. Our brain processes the information from the Golgi tendon organ, and this is how we experience the physical sensation of tension.

Tension is both an indicator and cause for physical stress. The stress could be good or useful, or the stress could cause the individual harm. In most instances, tension in the muscles causes movement and bending. This is minimal stress. However, the tension can also cause the body to seize and create aching or even sharp pain. Because we do not want to harm the individual, we will ignore the negative form of tension and stress. So, we can explore tension through the movement of the body within space. This movement can be exercise or simple circulation around a space and structure. However, we must focus on the constriction of the muscles; in the next form of touch: with stretch, we can focus on the pulling of the muscles.

Design can use tension by encouraging the individual to move. Movement requires the use of tension and compression to move the body through space. This movement will improve the user, but also accentuate and trace the space. In a time where there is too little exercise for much of the public, it is a good opportunity to push forward the sense of tension in design. How do we get people to move? We need attractors that pull people from standing or sitting. Visual and other sensory engagement is a possibility. Encouraging physical interaction through games, dancing, and sports is another. Moving people via vertical and horizontal circulation is yet another option, and stairs are a great way to get people to explore motion and tension.

Exploring design as only tension is theoretically interesting, because we would need to rely solely on movement. This is possible, and the movements would help describe the space, where the motion defines and fills the architecture. In this way, the motion can be classified and based on frequency, strength, and speed. This is a very Modern way to define a space, and the exercise can be taken so far as to nullify the need of spatial envelopes, where the movement of the body is the architecture.

If we were to design a space that did not incorporate tension, then the space would be static and dead. No movement would push us to ask whether the space was necessary at all. And, without space, there would be no tension, because there wouldn't be movement – movement creates space, because it gives purpose. Without movement and space, there is limited tension.

Tension can also be used for time, as tension is work that can be measured by time. Too much tension can cause injury or pain, and the body registers the amount and time of tension – not only through wear and soreness of the muscles, but also through pain and sweat. What does it mean to define a space with the body and then require it to hold the position to perpetuate the space? Is this the same as the movement? Actually, the exercise is the limitation of movement, not exacerbation of it.

To use tension in an existing space, we must limit a sedentary way of inhabiting the structure. Movement is both Modern and necessary, where we can make the user move to add interest for themselves. To add mystery and surprise around corners and up stairs is likely to improve movement. An existing space can have new material or amenities to draw people into it. What kind of narrative can the designer create to impel the user to move through the building – the structure is like a book. Social interaction can also attract people through or up into a structure – a person is much more willing to act when given the opportunity to have a friend to talk and interact with. Can we create moments throughout an existing structure where people can bump into each other and have a conversation? Can we have moments where individuals can exercise for exercise's sake?

It appears that tension is the motor for motion, and motion defines and changes a space. In this way, tension can be seen as creating space. As a sense, we understand tension can be measured to find the extent of motion through speed, frequency, and strength, and in turn, speed, frequency, and strength can measure a structure. Can we find a parallel or connection between the sense of tension and the physical, structural phenomenon of tension? Could they be the same? Should they be the same? We will want to explore similar ideas in the sense of stretch. The two senses are very much interrelated, but strangely, they use different sensors. Perhaps, both forms of sense can be used together, in parallel.

Tension Precedents

Create light, structurally minimal spaces.

Increase dimensions, area, or volume of object or space.

Fitting or shaping body (clothing).

Handrails and safety lines.

Elastic, rubber bands.

Exercise and athletic equipment.

Electrical and structural cabling.

Mechanical chains and belts.

Inflated structures, elements, and tires.

Springs.

Tension Possibilities

Divert attention from other stress.

Understand another's position or status.

Instruct how to complete physical action.

Augment and exceed inherent tensile capacity.

Alter shape of an element, space, or object.

Counter other tensile and compressive forces.

Examine and test capabilities.

Modify self.

Choreograph movement.

Contribute to other tension elements and agents.

Tension Sensors

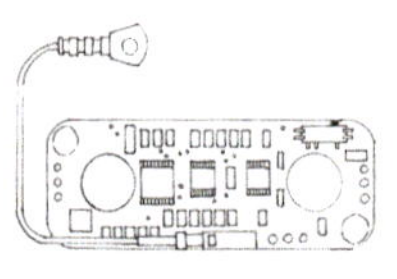

Muscle Sensor

Flex Sensor

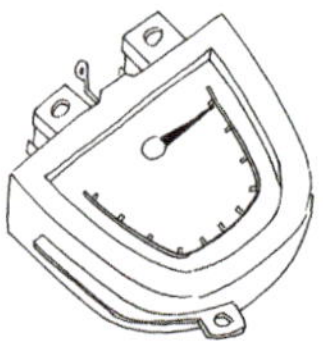

Tensiometer

Tension Actuators

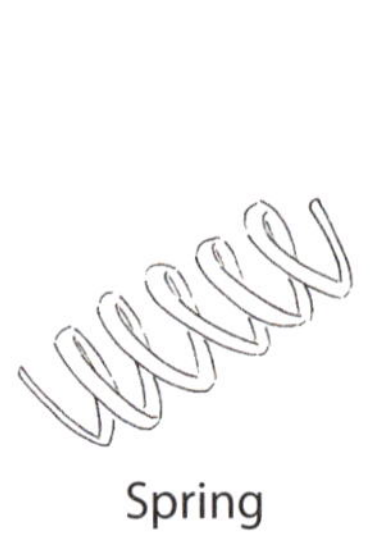

Spring

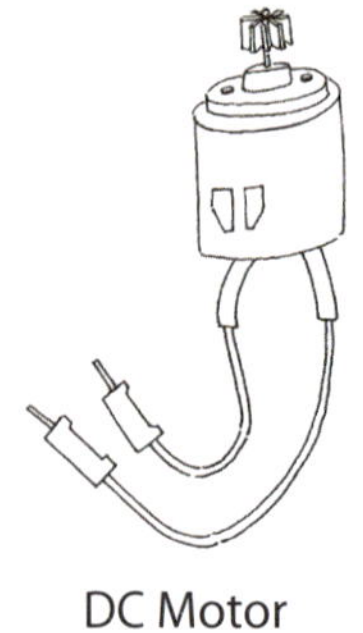

DC Motor

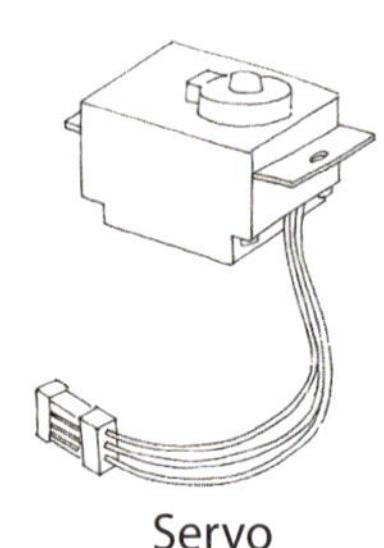

Servo

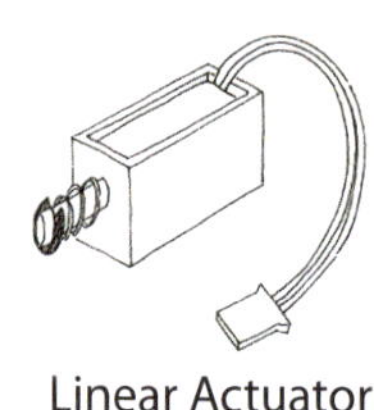

Linear Actuator

Tension Interpretations

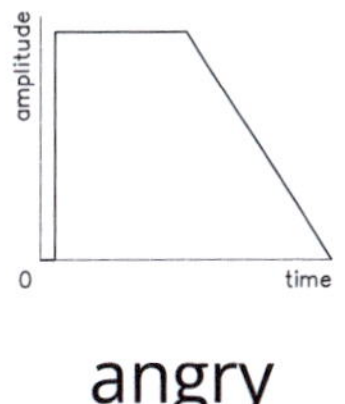

angry

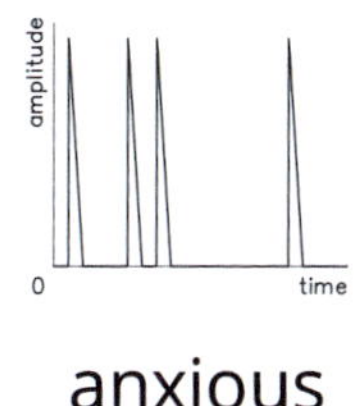

anxious

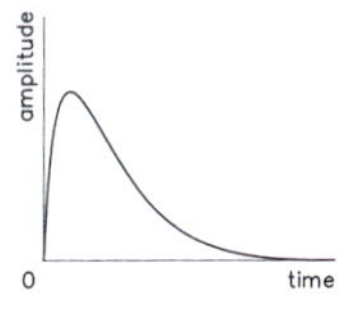

confident

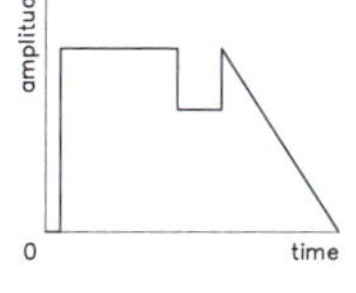

determined

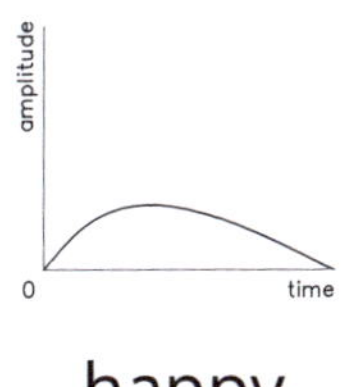

happy

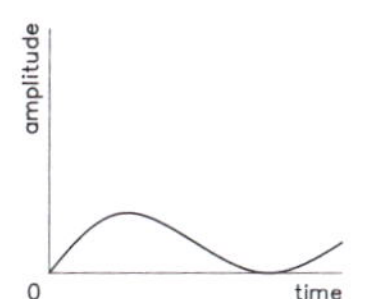

meditative

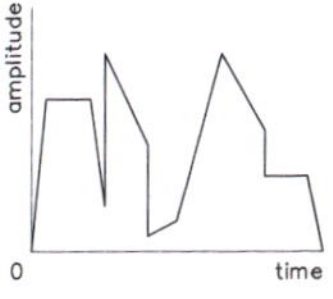

perplexed

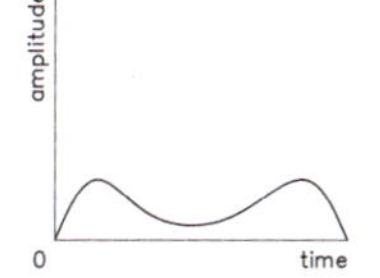

withdrawn

Touch: Stretch

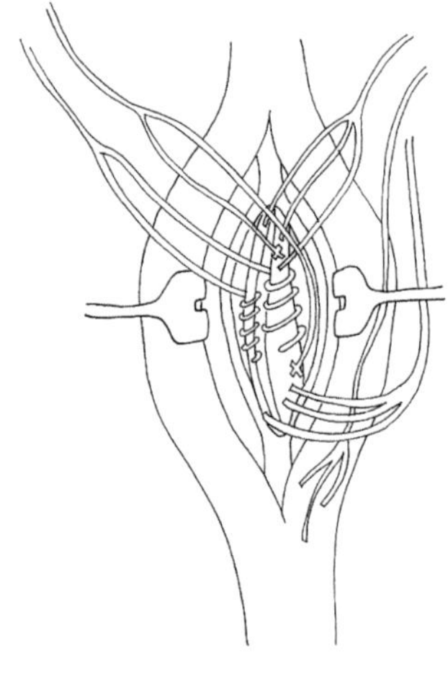

Muscle Spindle

The sense of stretch allows the body to register the pulling of the muscles with muscle spindles. Like tension, stretch indicates an amount of stress on the muscle. The stress can be too much to handle, but it can also be a beneficial stress to improve the body and allow it to understand its physical state. Stretch occurs when the body is extending itself beyond a normal or minimal range. The sensor ensures no harm and annunciates any issue. Because we are trying to use the senses to help design and not to injure, we will only look at use of stretch and the muscle spindle for good within our frame of design. Like tension, we will explore stretch through the movement of the body across space. Unlike tension, the exploration will not be through typical use of the space and structure, instead it will be through exercise and pulling the muscles beyond a standard range. For example, reaching overhead for an object on a shelf or down over a guardrail. So, like tension, it is about the movement of the body through space, and furthermore, it is exploring the limits of the body in space as well as the limits of the space.

We can use the design installation to encourage the body to stretch beyond its normal limits. Again, this is not meant to be an exploration of pain, so it is a controlled extension to and beyond normal limits. How do we make individuals exercise and stretch? We need to draw them toward attractions and those attractions should be near the limits of reach. Up, down, and beyond obstructions, such as gates, rails, and furniture. What are they reaching for? What do they want? Physical and social interaction, exercise, food and drink, and entertainment are all viable reasons, and this is likely where the designer should push the concept of stretch in a design installation.

As with tension, exploring design as only stretch is enticing and would rely on the limits of movement. However, we would need to utilize tension and proprioception to reach those limits. Therefore, being strictly stretch is not likely possible, yet we should use these other senses to reach the limits and define a space as well as define the body within the space. The sense of stretch would be variable with a plateau which we would not want to meet, as this is the realm of overextension and pain. Using exercise, such as yoga to understand the limits allows the individual to know themselves physically, but it would also allow the one exercising to know how to index the limits of the body in space, defining the realm of use and the margins.

To design without the use of stretch would entail the lack of movement, and all dynamism in the project is lost. This is not ideal, and as mentioned in tension, without some extent of stretch, the use of space is not required, because there is no movement, and therefore the design would be flat, lacking depth and roundness. What is the purpose in such a space? Why would we do this?

Beyond the movement to and beyond limits, stretch can also be used to communicate. To stretch is to provide a small amount of stress, and the stress can be coded as a signal or even a language to share information. One can use something like Morse code or the simple introduction of the sense to amplify other information or senses, such as stretch to add import to aural information or to provide an announcement of danger or change. Although the experience of stretch is variable, we can treat it as binary, unless we can translate the extent of the sense. This variability adds one dimension which can provide the magnitude of the information. Otherwise, the coding will be simply off and on.

Using stretch in an existing space requires the designer to survey the space for the areas just out of reach, such as stairways, open expanses, and areas overhead. Pairing stretch with other senses to provide impetus to use the sense is a fine combination, complementing one sensory experience with another. Again, we must have attractions or moments of interest that encourage the user to stretch, and these are surely given through the use of other senses. Interaction with others requires other forms of touch, hearing, and vision. Exercise requires proprioception, multiple forms of touch, and often hearing or vision. Entertainment can use a large range of senses, but the question is what is the entertainment that requires stretch? A good precedent is seeing over others in a crowd during a presentation or performance. But, what are other examples we can use?

If tension is the motor for motion, stretch is the boundary of motion. Really, it is stretch that defines the space, when not relying on vision, and tension through motion may create the space, it is stretch that sets the limits. With use, we are able to extend beyond the limits, and we grow and change, the index of these limits provides the definition of the growth and change.

Stretch Precedents

Physical movement – flexibility.

Clothing.

Exercise.

Surfaces over frame – space.

Surfaces over frame – furniture.

Surfaces over frame – equipment.

Medical equipment.

Fabric.

Exercise equipment.

Ornamentation.

Stretch Possibilities

Resist shortening or withdrawal.

Direct movement.

Move body parts.

Lower air or fluid pressure.

Alter environment as diversion.

Increase physical capability and stretch.

Reminder of task or event.

Draw attention to part or element.

Warning.

Translate and map other sensory input.

Stretch Sensors

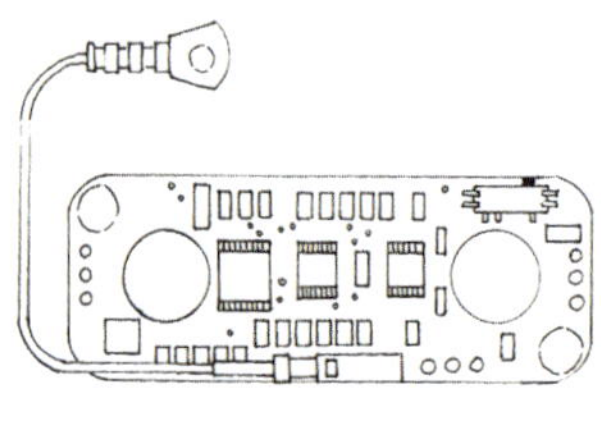

Muscle Sensor

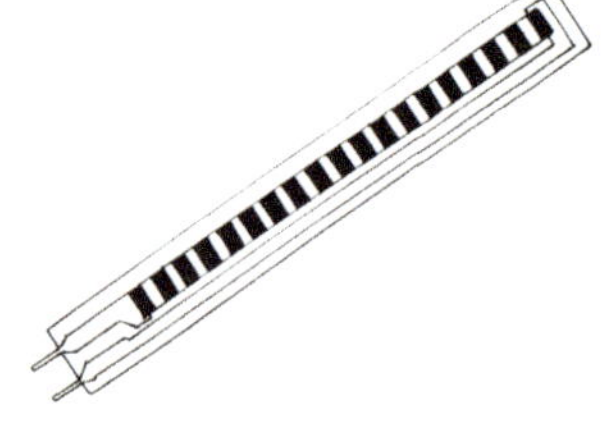

Flex Sensor

Stretch Actuators

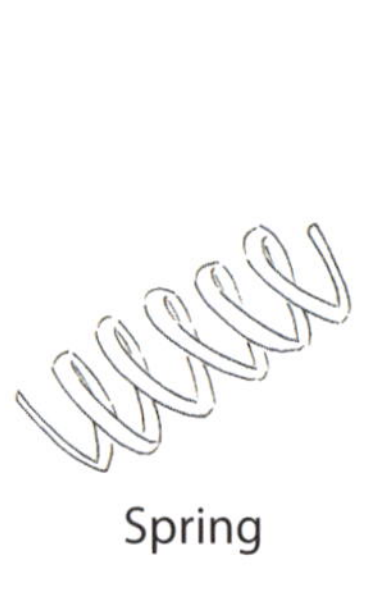

Spring

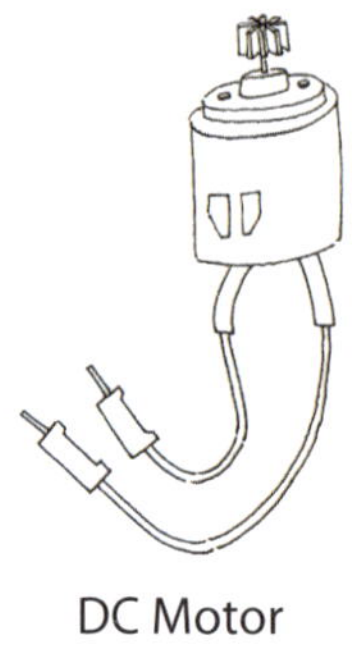

DC Motor

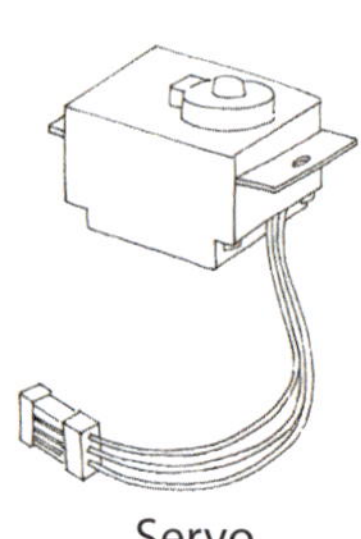

Servo

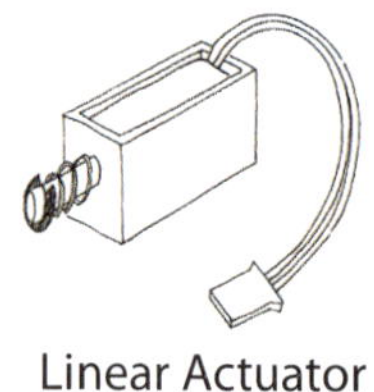

Linear Actuator

Stretch Interpretations

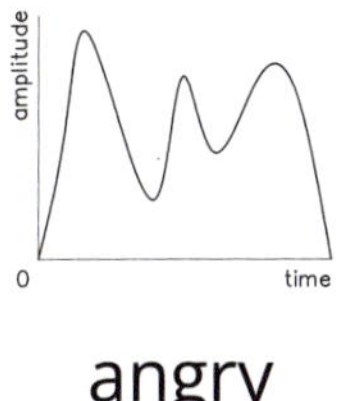

angry

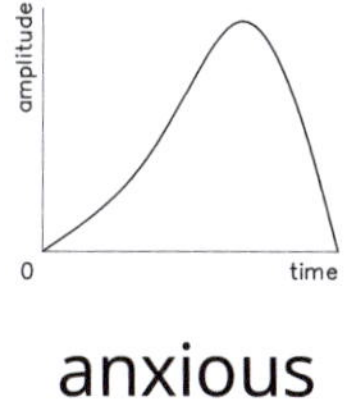

anxious

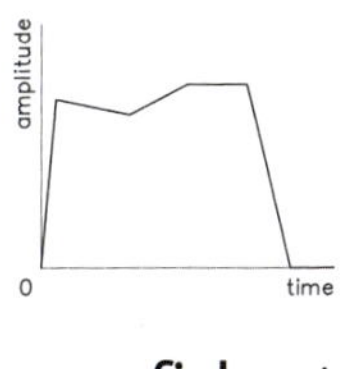

confident

determined

happy

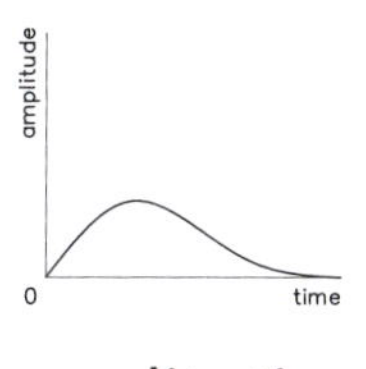

meditative

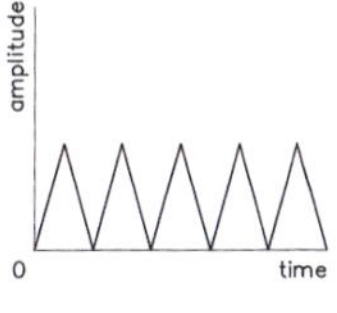

perplexed

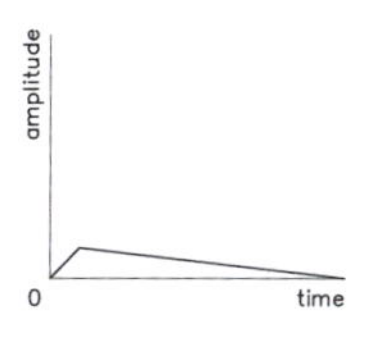

withdrawn

Touch: Vibration

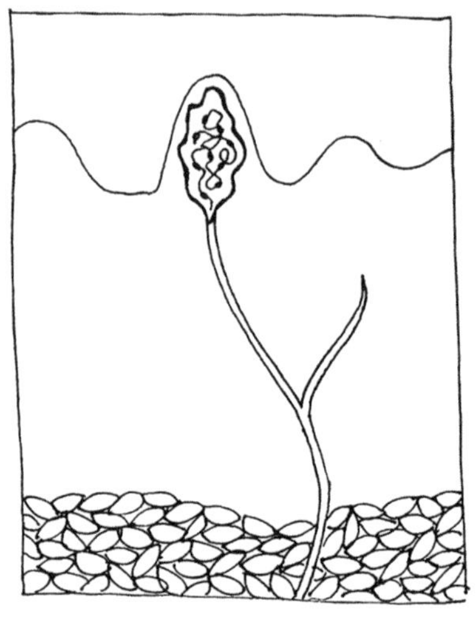

Meissner Corpuscle

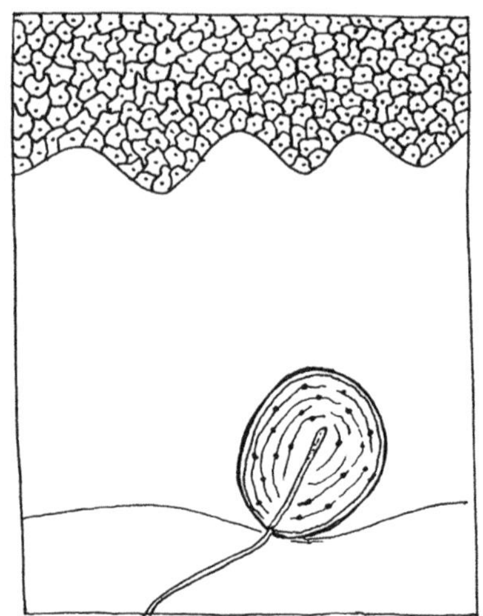

Pacinian Corpuscle

The Meissner corpuscle and the Pacinian corpuscle sense vibration. As mentioned previously, the Meissner corpuscle is a type of mechanoreceptor, a sensory nerve ending that is sensitive to mechanical pressure or movement. When an object comes into contact with the skin, the movement or pressure of the object activates the Meissner corpuscle, which sends a signal to the brain that is interpreted as a sensation of touch or vibration. This allows the body to detect and respond to stimuli in the environment, such as the movement of an object against the skin or the variation of pressure against the body.

The Pacinian corpuscle is also a type of mechanoreceptor, and like the Meissner corpuscle, it is sensitive to mechanical pressure or movement. When an object comes into contact with the skin, the movement or pressure of the object activates the Pacinian corpuscle, which sends a signal to the brain that is interpreted as a sensation of touch or vibration. This allows the body to detect and respond to stimuli in the environment, such as the movement of an object against the skin or the pressure of a surface against the body. Unlike the Meissner corpuscle, which is sensitive to low-frequency vibrations, the Pacinian corpuscle is most sensitive to high-frequency vibrations. This allows it to detect rapid changes in pressure or movement, such as those that occur when an object is rapidly tapped against the skin.

Vibration makes the static come alive through the dispersion of sound or a periodic wave through a surface or solid. Naturally, vibration is created through movement, and it can be used as a form of communication, threat, or as a by-product of motion. As with other senses and types of touch, vibration is best experienced in limited amounts, as vibration in a constantly moving environment would be lost. A still space will allow the sense of vibration to reverberate and nearly broadcast through a space. Using vibration allows variables of amplitude, speed, and constancy or intermittence.

Vibration allows the communication of information without the need for other senses. On the other hand, the sense of vibration will augment and complement the other senses. Most of the time in practice, vibration is used to alert the user to some change or notification. Using a vibrating motor that rotates eccentrically is the most common way to create vibration in electronic devices, and it is common on phones, videogame controllers, and even apparel to convey meaning. However, another use is the change in quantity or quality over time. This could be useful or annoying, as the vibration signal is continuous with variation. Nonetheless, the advantage is that others never have to see or hear the information, the wearer can feel it, instead.

If design were only vibration, information would need to be communicated through various vibrating motors or using the amplitude, frequency, and intermittence to provide information. This could be confusing with a cacophony of vibration. On the other hand, the absolute silence of a space lacking any sensory vibration would be eerie and unnerving. A path of moderation is preferred. Fewer vibration sources will help improve the efficacy of the sense.

Most designs do not incorporate vibration, so there is little to lose without the use of vibration. But, the introduction of the sense in an installation will create a more dynamic effect where the project has a nervous energy that creates depth in an otherwise flattened design. Without vibration, the designer really needs to have varying intensities in the other senses to create the innervating effect of vibration. Weathering and detail work will allow a visual analogy to vibrating, and the repetition of other senses will give a similar feeling. Can other senses vibrate? Sound is vibration. And, the variation of the sound and its many characteristics will allow vibration. The pulsing of taste or smell will create a vibration, and some might say the use of hot sauces can provide such a sensation.

Vibration can be more than a sense of touch. We can use the same method of vibration to put water or air into motion. With light and optics, this can create shimmering and almost magical effects. Furthermore, the use of sound through the vibration of magnets in speakers can create mesmerizing forms with ferrofluid, a liquid with iron suspended within. Similarly, complementing vibration to sound in headphones or headrests can create a buzzing vision in the user, as the head moves slightly back and forth.

To use vibration in an existing structure, the designer should remove environmental indicators and substitute these with vibration. There can be multiple types of vibrating–intermittent or varying over time, like a gradient. In addition, vibration can serve as a warning in areas that are not appropriate for access. Otherwise, care should be taken to only use vibration where information needs to be conveyed, and the user needs to understand the code or meaning of the vibration. Is it a coded language? Is it a cultural known? Vibration can give meaning in many ways. What is the best one to use in an existing space?

The designer must use vibration's variables, including amplitude, frequency, and the constant or varying signal to improve the built environment. The designer should keep in mind the meaning and use of the sense of vibration in the installation's context in order to communicate with as many users as possible. A light touch is needed in order to avoid overexposure to the sense, and with care, vibration will allow a richer design, without being kitsch or inappropriate.

Vibration Precedents

Phone alert.

Vibration to set and remove air in concrete.

Game controllers to simulate action.

Muscle therapy.

Testing and sensing integrity and material qualities, as well as natural disasters (earthquakes, hurricanes, and tornadoes).

Nerve therapy.

Toys.

Locomotion (Hex Bugs, Electric Football).

Insect communication.

Deterrent – pet pads.

Vibration Possibilities

Map other sense, such as vision, hearing, touch, time, and chemoreception.

Alert when danger or object approaching.

Directionality – hot and cold, relative direction.

Convey information along a solid.

Mapping site with info overlay.

Hazard/boundary warning.

Coach behavior (limbs, posture, pressure).

Locomotion.

Mimic touch.

Create motion in liquid.

Vibration Sensors

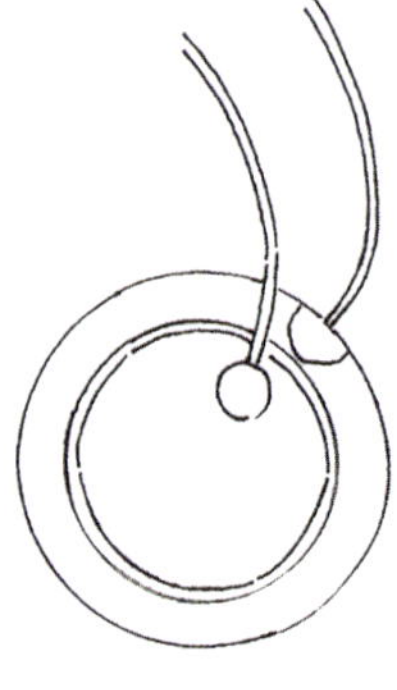

Piezo Element

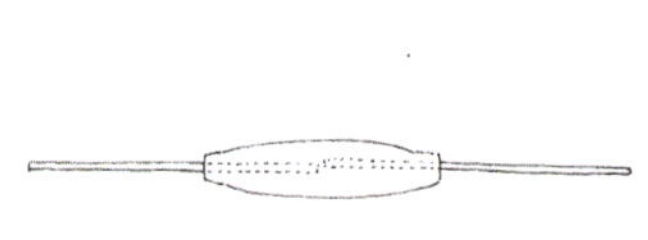

Reed Switch

Vibration Actuators

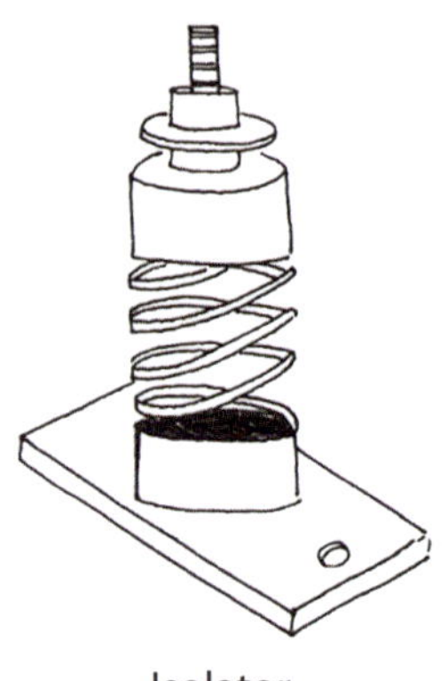

Isolator

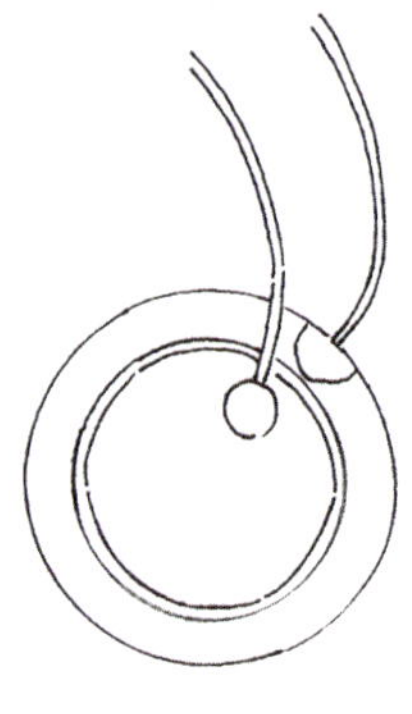

Piezo Element

Vibration Interpretations

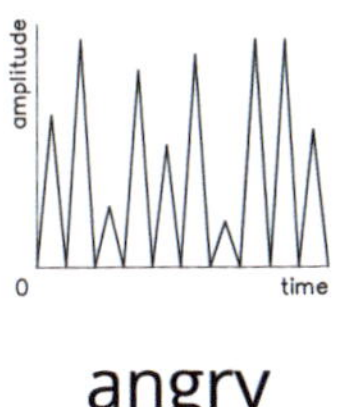

angry

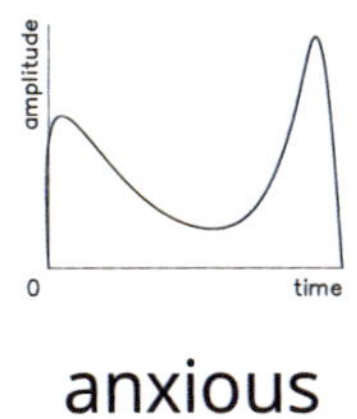

anxious

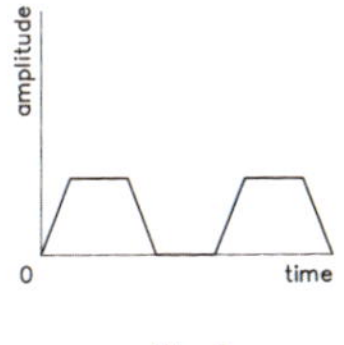

confident

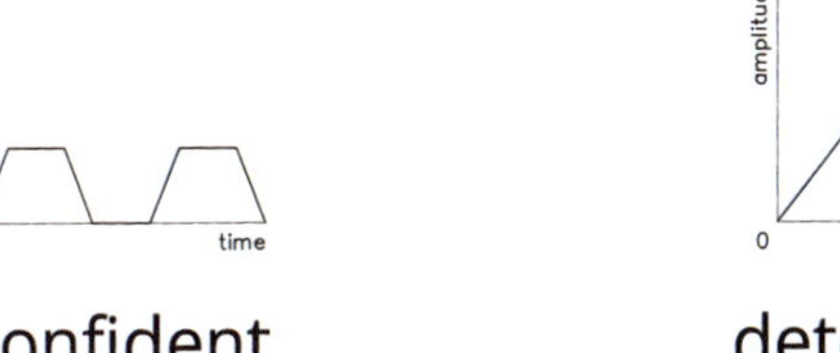

determined

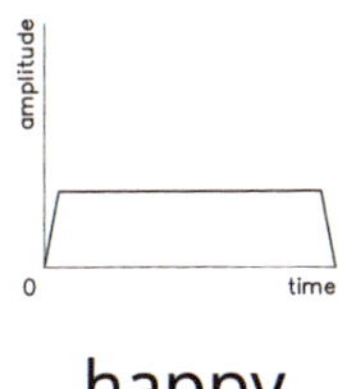

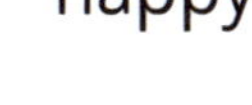

happy

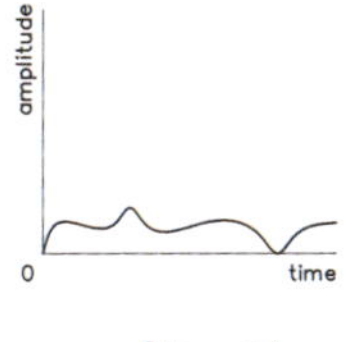

meditative

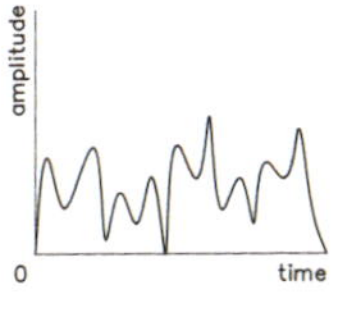

perplexed

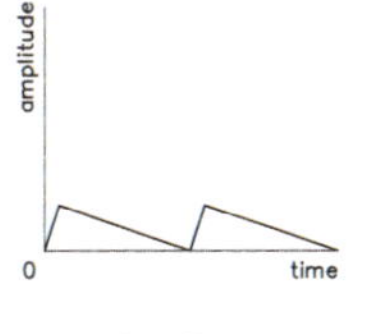

withdrawn

Equilibrioception

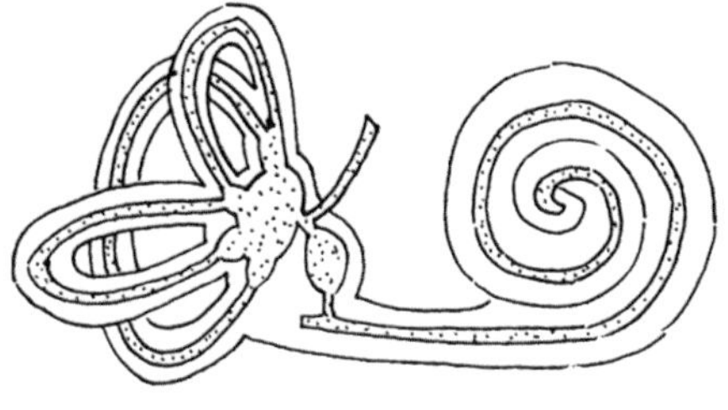

Inner Ear

The vestibular system is located in the inner ear. This system allows balance and provides a sense of directionality. It does this by measuring the acceleration and orientation of the head and then sending signals to the brain which coordinates movement and maintains balance. The vestibular system includes a network of channels filled with fluid as well as tiny hairs that extend into the fluid. When the head moves, the fluid moves along with it, causing the hairs to bend. The hair bending activates sensory cells, which send signals to the brain that are used to calculate the head's motion and direction. The brain translates the stimuli to orchestrate the body's movement and maintain balance.

Design can use the sense of equilibrioception to create a more interesting interaction with a structure or installation. We can make the body move and contort by changing the elevation and angle of walls, floors, stairs, and ramps. However, we must be careful not to throw off the user so much that there is tripping or falling. In addition, we can increase the effects to equilibrioception by using visual cues, so even the ceiling and elements out of reach of the body can be altered and changed to create a visual, sympathetic response.

Equilibrioception is rarely used in design, other than amusement attractions. The attractions effectively use the sense, and they can be a hint as to how to use the sense in other instances. Taking stairs up or down can create a sensation of turning and swirling. Allowing the floor to undulate up and down will make the body feel as if it is bobbing. Other ways we can use equilibrioception is to move the head. How can we make the head go into motion? Turning, lowering, and raising by creating visual or aural interest is one way. However, we can also force the body into other positions, such as described with proprioception.

If design were only using the sense of equilibrioception, then it would create a surprising, mysterious, yet possibly nauseating experience, because the body would not know what the next movement might be without some foresight using vision or similar. As such, there are several ways to make the body feel the sense of equilibrioception. These include: rapid translation through space, rotation, change in elevation, and a combination of these. The permutations of the possible combinations would be: translation and rotation, translation and elevation change, as well as rotation and elevation change. Each of these permutations would create a different feeling and possibly a different emotion.

As mentioned above, most design doesn't include equilibrioception, so it would not be surprising to not see the sense in an installation. However, if it is to be included, the designer needs to be very careful about how the integration of the sense is accomplished, because the use without a clear narrative would seem gimmicky and odd. We should be sure that the movement of the body is appropriate with the design intent.

Some alternative uses of equilibrioception include communication of emotions, ideas, and even language. We can affect emotion with the understanding or translation of movement to convey a feeling. For example, moving upward can create the feeling of suspense and inevitability, whereas to fall can make the user feel foreboding and anxiety. Another way the sense can create feelings is to move forward, creating the feeling of progress, and in opposite, moving backward can create a feeling of frustration and regression. Rotation can also create feelings of exhilaration, or with too much speed, a sense of inebriation or loss of orientation. Then, there are several combinations which can provoke different emotions. For example, to revolve and raise can create the sense of elation, while revolving and falling can create a fateful emotion. Revolving and movement together can create a sense of confusion and loss of control, whereas the movement up and down while moving forward or backward can evoke the emotional feelings of a story, like a rollercoaster running its course.

We are able to change an existing structure to create moments of equilibrioception by speeding or slowing the movement of the body through the space. This can include changing the speed of an elevator, but it could also be the encouragement of the user to move swiftly up or down a stair by drawing the eye and interest through the vertical circulation. This can occur with varying or changing points of interest, morphing ornament, or access to exterior or interior moments of action or change. Furthermore, we can accentuate the shape of a space by changing the elevation or face of floors and walls to create physical adjustments as the body moves through the space.

Ultimately, equilibrioception can be one of the most visceral senses to design with because it makes the body change its position and orientation in space. This change conveys or evokes emotion, which will affect the user. The designer needs to ensure there is a clear intent or narrative otherwise the use of equilibrioception can seem cheap or inappropriate. However, with careful application, equilibrioception will be an amazing source of interest and experience. More design should use the sense of equilibrioception – it does not only need to be for rides and attractions.

Equilibrioception Precedents

Amusement rides.

Play equipment.

Vehicle movement.

Body movement.

Furniture positions and orientation.

Training for physical activities.

Exercising.

Sea, Car, and Air Sickness.

Body position relative to gravity.

Counter sense of dizziness.

Equilibrioception Possibilities

Entertainment.

Mimic movement.

Confuse.

Augment perception.

Communicate ideas and feelings.

Encourage direction of movement.

Counter discomfort and movement.

Therapy.

Augment movement.

Communicate feelings or concepts.

Equilibrioception Sensors

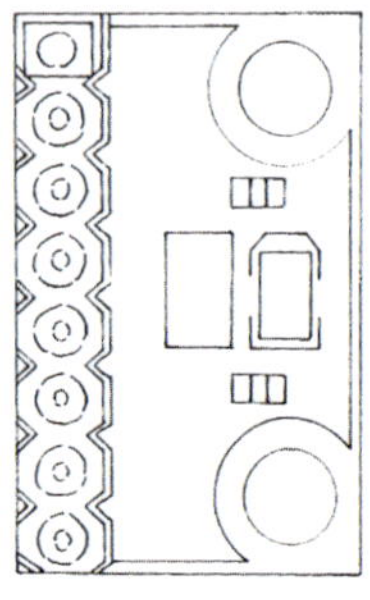

Accelerometer

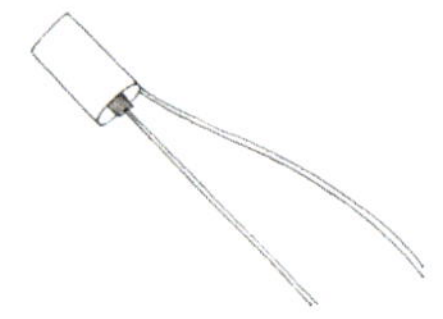

Tilt Sensor

Equilibrioception Actuators

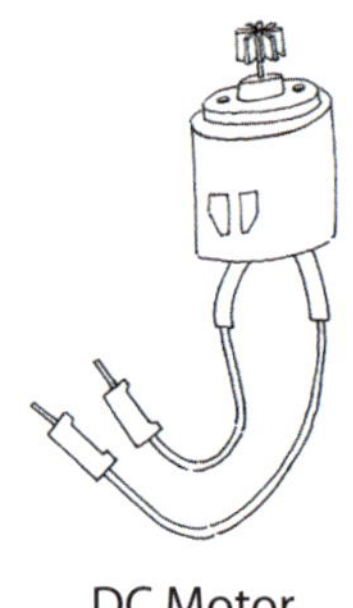

DC Motor

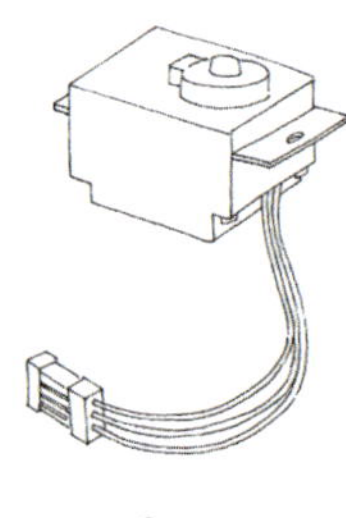

Servo

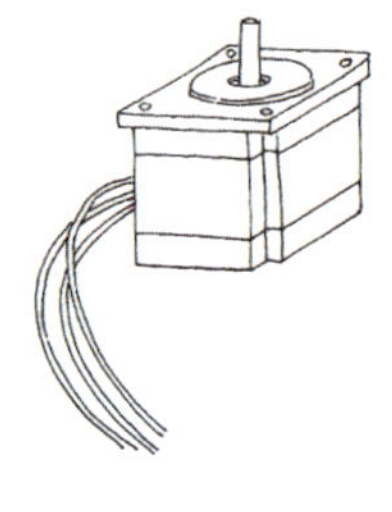

Stepper Motor

Equilibrioception Interpretations

shaking
turning
dropping
erratic movement
undulation

angry

rapid movement
tilting
random motion
moments of calm
great acceleration

anxious

rhythmic motion
continuous speed
steady direction
faster than context
slow acceleration

confident

high acceleration
high velocity
fluid motion
smooth transitions
minimal variation

determined

inertia
slow changes
smooth movement
long cycles of motion
continuous velocity

happy

minimal movement
continuous acceleration
slow turning
upward motion
periodic change

meditative

randomness
change in direction
varying velocity
rotation in all directions
erratic movement

perplexed

apparent stasis
subtle acceleration
minimal angular movement
long pauses
occasional activity from context

withdrawn

Sound

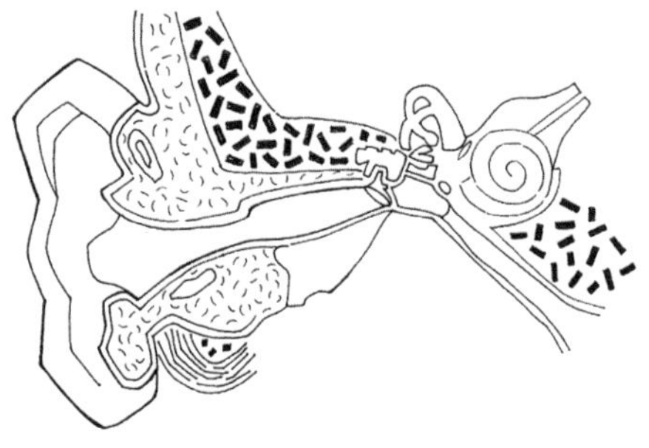

Ear

Sound is detected and processed by the auditory system, which includes the ears, the auditory nerves, and the brain. When sound enters the ear, the eardrum vibrates, and this vibration is transmitted to the bones in the middle ear (the malleus, incus, and stapes), and it goes to the cochlea, a spiral-shaped structure deep in the inner ear. Inside the cochlea, the vibrations are converted into electrical signals that pass to the brain via the auditory nerve, then the brain processes these signals and interprets them as sound.

Hearing, like vision is a sense that operates well at distance. Although it is slower and weaker than light in sending information through air, sound travels through the medium to get to the ear. Sound also travels very well through other liquids and solids. It moves through the vibration of matter, and liquids and solids have higher densities than air and other gases, which allows a more efficient transfer of the wave energy. As such, we can hear sound through materials, not just through air. In fact, sound is more efficient through dense materials, and we must be careful not to injure our ears with over-powerful transmissions, such as pinging in water.

We use hearing to intake information and sounds in order to better understand the world. Often, we use it in combination with other senses, or we can use it alone, in lieu of vision and others. Sound provides meaning without a need for light. Not only do we receive sounds from specific sources, but we also take in the sound of the context and conditions. Reverberation tells us the make up and size of spaces, while the milieu of sounds expresses environmental conditions.

Similar to vision, hearing is always on when awake. Although hearing can be passive, hearing incidental sounds, hearing is almost entirely active. However, we are able to block out sound with our brains and can even sleep through commotion, and our brains are able to filter out the sense to focus on other signals or tasks.

We use hearing wherever we use vision. However, we can also utilize hearing without sight, and it is nearly as efficient as relying on the visual, though full physical definition is more difficult to discern. When used in concert with vision, a very clear understanding is given, only made better by touch, in most instances.

For some, hearing and listening are the greatest skills. Some get lost in music or the sonic landscape, and they can pick out specific characteristics and sounds without trouble. For others, hearing is a secondary mode to understand the world, which is also very effective in concert with other senses, such as touch and vision.

We are able to affect how people hear by masking or blocking sound, enhancing sound, or combining sound to create new possibilities. These options give new experiential moments. As mentioned above, we are able to use our sense of hearing to understand the size and contents of a space as well as define what entities are nearby, but our ability to listen also allows us to receive spoken language, which is similar to written language for vision.

Manipulating sound electronically or using acoustical mechanisms, we can change how people hear and also what they hear. However, we are also able to adjust sonic experience by manipulating our ears and hearing. People who wear headphones or hearing aids are able to filter out the environment and only experience portions of the world of sound. Many of these devices are able to adjust pitch and amplitude, meaning anyone wearing one will have a different experience than those without. The sonic landscape can also be changed with various effects such as filtering, reverberation, and delay. These three can change the nature of a space, because they can limit the frequencies experienced, as well as augment or diminish the experiential size of the space just with adjusting the qualities of the sound.

We transform the signal in our minds through associating the sound with some value or memory. These relationships come naturally from our existence in the environment or the repetitive introduction of the signal over time. As mentioned above, removing sound affects the listener, but we can also use additive design to create new sonic experiences. Our brain can understand a new meaning from overlaying multiple sounds. In fact, this is the way many movie makers create new sounds for their films. The content of a movie is affected tremendously by what is heard, and the quality of these sounds can improve or lower the quality of the film's perception.

Sounds can be considered good, bad, or neutral, but we can also place a meaning on them by associating values. Producing the sound multiple times in connection with another object or entity, we are able to create new connotations. We can also affect the memory of a sound be repetition of the sound during the experience of some event or input from another sense.

Hearing is used nearly constantly throughout the day, and sound enhances other senses and emotions. Most people will preference the visual when traversing the environment, but sound is a great indicator, and many things in our world signal or can be sensed through sound. The sense works at a distance, but there is a disparity in the speed of the signal of sound and of light, and the two quickly separate over distance creating silent visual events and later disembodied sounds that may match or differ greatly with the perceived image. Nevertheless, sound is extremely useful in our day to day lives and throughout history, as we accept language first aurally and second visually. Language is believed to have come from sounds from individuals long before the written word. As such, it may be intrinsic and atavistic to our working brains.

We use hearing to create memory and understanding in our lives, as well as to apply, analyze, and evaluate the world in order to create and thrive. It is crucial that we create these memories of sound in order to provide a description of the object and use this understanding to create meaning that acts as a catalyst or stimulus to put us into action. With this, we can think about how the thing emanating sound works or acts and later judge how it can be used or avoided. Finally, with the mastery of the sound and hearing in general, we can intuit new sonic signals when moving through a novel space.

Hearing may not be our first or primary sense, but it is extremely useful to navigate the world. In some situations, it may be our only sense that allows us to be safe and interact with the environment. Because it is such an intrinsic and important sense, we draw associations through specific sounds, and these may be shared from culture to culture or may be very different. However, the quality and form of the sound provides information that can be shared across populations and languages. In some instances, it is possible and maybe even important to impart meaning on something, such as an alarm or the buzzing of a hornet, in order to exist safely.

The sense of hearing is useful, but it can overpower the user and muddle meaning when combined with other sensory input. As with other senses, it is best to start with no or minimal sound and build up. One of the beautiful things about sound is that it can describe three-dimensional space and directionality. So, multiple outputs or speakers are suggested when working with sound design. These outputs can be linked with systems like Dolby Surround Sound, or the sounds can be from multiple independent sources to create a mélange. Even with the multiple sounds, each should start at a low volume and increased to the desired amplitude, however the sound volume can vary from source to source and could even change over time.

Some music producers talk about making space in compositions. This is the use of silence to enhance the music. Even the best sonic signal can be monotonous or overpowering when played too long, so rests or pauses in what is heard is very helpful to create structure and understanding, while the variation provides interest. Even a single sound or voice should be separated with pauses to create an aural rhythm that will satisfy the user. Sometimes what is not heard is as important as that which is heard.

If we only designed with hearing, we would have a rich spatial environment, but the limited sensory input would provide one or very few inputs if trying to convey information. So, sound requires a hierarchy and maybe even a mode of interaction. If a design requires call and response, the user must understand when and how to interject with the system. If a design has one source producing or controlling the sound, then how will the user be able to interact with others and with the source? The system should easily allow the listener to interact or at least react to the source of the sound.

If design did not include hearing, how easily could individuals interact? Every environment has sound, and it is nearly impossible not to hear or create sound when moving through a space. The absence of sound would ensure the other senses are front and center. But, the order or hierarchy of a design might not be apparent without sound, though it is much more likely that the absence of vision would make an impediment of a structure.

Some alternative senses for hearing would be sight, but also smell and touch. All of these can provide multi-dimensional experiences, especially when they are used in combination. Oppositely, if we want to create a personal experience with sound, it is possible to limit the dimensionality of the sound by experiencing the sense through a liquid or solid medium. The vibration of the sound waves requires mass to allow the noise to propagate, and as mentioned before liquid and solid materials are very good and efficient means to broadcast. However, the listener must be in contact with the medium, in order to hear the sound, and the source of the sound seems to come from the body part that is touching the medium. This creates a very close and intimate experience.

An environment can be augmented with sound, but we must keep in mind the method. Locating places and objects from which sound will emanate is good, but we must tastefully develop the sonic environment with low volume, building these up, then adjusting the frequency of the sound to better engage with the space. Each space has a specific frequency and resonance, as well as other acoustical properties, and the designer can use these to grab the listener's attention. When the specific frequency is hit, a space seems to buzz and come to life, tottering and rumbling. When the designer uses the existing space's acoustical properties, the designer creates a stronger bond between the new design elements and the existing environment. A tall space with hard surfaces will give a very active sonic landscape, with echoing, reverberation, and delay. A small, padded space will feel intimate and quiet.

Design is a reiterative act, and the architect would want to evaluate the sound work developed in order to improve or build upon the soundscape. Because this is likely a qualitative evaluation, the designer should determine if one sound state is better, the same, or worse than another. If the state is better, then it is likely the architect will want to keep it, but if it is worse, then what should be done? A new sound or audio source should be tried, tested, and evaluated, and then another, if necessary. If a state continues to be worse than the original or the highest use, then it may very well be likely that the environment does not need such a sound experience.

Sound Precedents

Music.

Speech / Communication (Words).

Alarms, reminders.

Entertainment, sound design (movies, music, television).

Movement and tones to describe change of objects.

Environmental sounds.

Mark characteristics of health (blood pressure, breathing, etc.).

Metal detector; Geiger counter.

Underline emotion (tone, timbre).

Mechanical parts and operation.

Sound Possibilities

Define/design aural character of a space (active acoustics).

Analyze size and materials of a space or object (echolocation, acoustics).

Map information to monitor while using another sense.

Announce boundaries and spatial change.

Active diversion, entertainment, response to local environment.

Create emotional response (sub-aural and very high-pitched sound).

Mark passage of time and / or space.

Movement and augmentation of at specific frequency.

Calm and engage with tonal / harmonic.

Atomize and create forms using sound waves in water and other liquids.

Sound Sensors

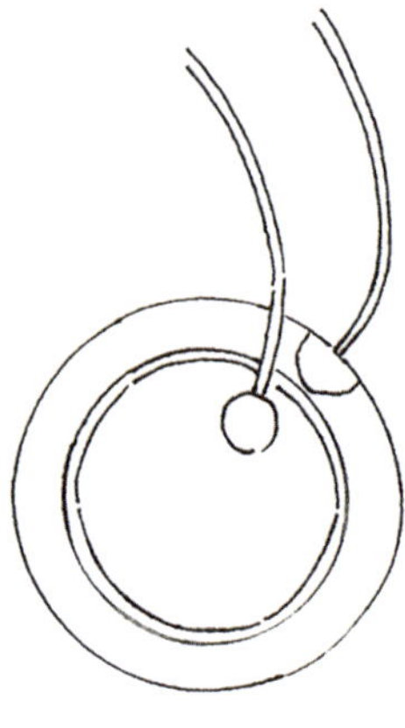

Piezo Element

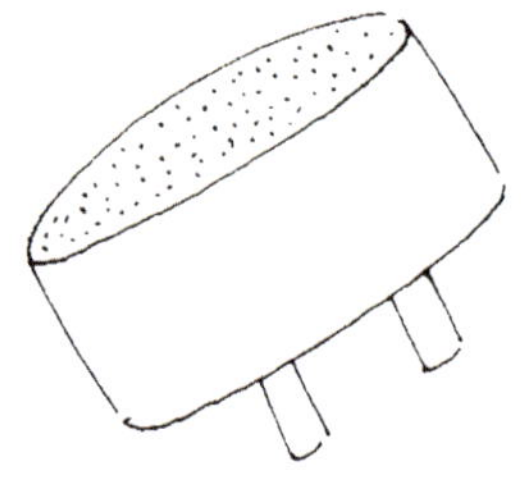

Microphone

Sound Actuators

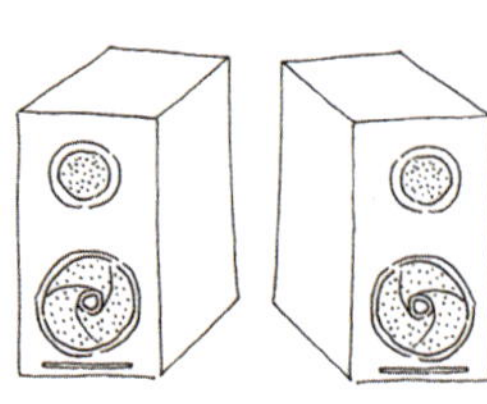

Speakers

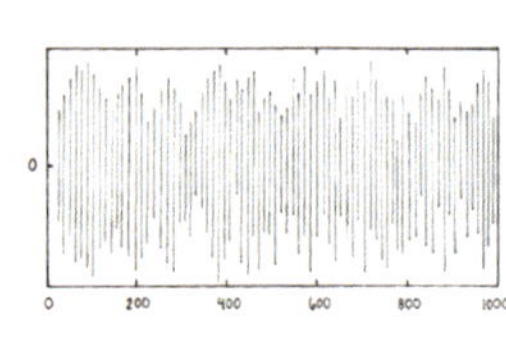

White Noise

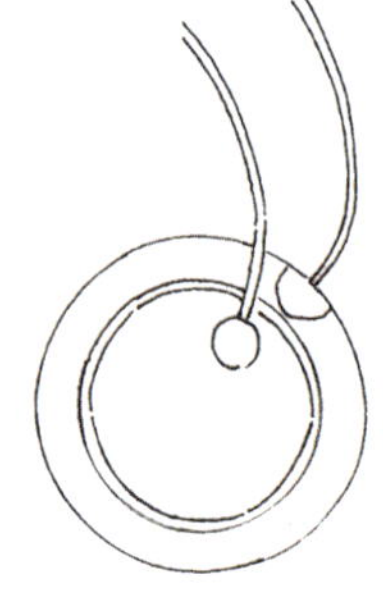

Piezo Element

Sound Interpretations

loud
artificially created
high-pitched
continuous
unintelligible

angry

reverberation
poor clarity
random spacing
occasional loud output
information rich

anxious

harmony
strong rhythm
long tones and sound
simple
developing and evolving

confident

pulse rate
melody following rhythm
rising themes and tones
balanced sound spectrum
moderate volume

determined

low volume
variation in audio spectrum
sounds from nature
rhythmic
optimistic

happy

comforting
evolving
wordless
developed low frequencies
long

meditative

stochastic
complex structure
varying spectral emphasis
pauses
weak transitions

perplexed

single sound source
filtered
low volume
delay
minor or descending

withdrawn

Smell

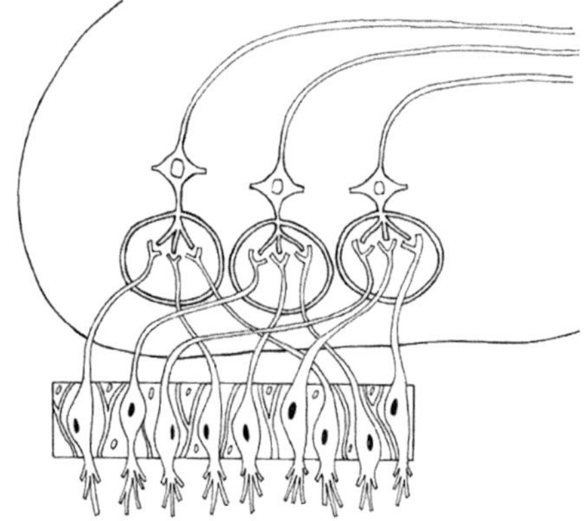

Olfactory Receptors

Olfactory receptors are specialized sensory cells that are located in the nose. They are responsible for detecting and identifying different smells. When we breathe in air, the air molecules enter our nose and dissolve in a layer of mucus that covers the olfactory receptors. The introduction of the molecules activates various olfactory receptors, which send signals to the brain that are interpreted as a sensation of smell. The brain then uses this information to identify the specific smell that we are experiencing. There are many different types of olfactory receptors, each of which is sensitive to different types of molecules. Furthermore, the combination of olfactory receptors provide the experience of a wide range of smells. We have evolved these receptors to determine the presence of specific chemicals to ensure health and wellbeing, but we can now use the receptors for enjoyment and understanding, beyond the physical requirement to sense dangerous materials and compounds.

Scent works at distance like vision and hearing, but scent has another dimension, in that the complex compounds seem to last longer in the environment to be experienced than lighter compounds, which deteriorate quickly. Most scents are complicated and have multiple compounds, and the proportion of these creates a signature smell, so two materials may have similar chemicals, but one has more than or a slight variation from the other, then the smell will be different, if the human nose can recognize the compounds. We are able to smell many thousands of chemicals, but other species can sense more, so it is understandable that some animals will have a better or different understanding of the elements in the environment than we do. Nevertheless, scent is an extremely important sense that transmits information, but it is commonly overlooked for vision and hearing.

Through evolution, we have developed the sense of smell to detect materials, however we can now use the sense to convey information. We are able to create and capture smells through perfumes, essential oils, reduction, and other methods. These can be used for specific knowledge, especially along cultural lines. Some groups have special meaning associated with certain smells, and this knowledge allows us to use these smells as signals or warnings.

Because of the bias toward vision and even hearing, we do not often think of using smell in design, except perhaps cooking. However, as architects, we should. Scents and memories are very closely related. When we smell, the olfactory bulb, which is responsible for analyzing smells in the brain, is close to the amygdala and hippocampus (the regions of the brain responsible for retaining memories), many smells overlap with memories, and memories easily can be triggered with a specific smell.

There are cultural aspects to utilizing smells in urban and environmental design, as well. For every different city and region, there are common smells that the area is accustomed to, and there are many different smells that the area or community has never grown fond of. Knowing each community is essential to create living spaces that will be liked. For example, a person from Chicago, Illinois may be accustomed to the smell of their environment and genuinely enjoy the aroma of the streets, but a tourist from Paris, France might smell the area and dislike it immediately. Preference of smells pertaining to a community can be as specific as between counties or cities in the same state or as general as between nations or ethnicities.

Smell is similar to taste, touch, hearing, and vision in the case that the sense provides information about an object or space. In addition, smell is similar to vision and hearing because it can be transmitted over a distance. However, smell is different than the other senses in that it can determine precise chemicals, and the brain must rely on memory and intrinsic knowledge to determine what those chemicals mean. Other senses, besides taste, can provide an understanding on the size and motion of an entity, but smell and taste cannot.

Because scent has such charged meaning, one should use the sense to either attract or repel, although it can also be used to create moments of variation in a space. However, it is important to limit the amount of the odor to ensure it does not annoy or put off the user. Because smell carries memory and specific knowledge, it should be limited in scope to defined locations and groups. For example, rich floral perfumes are appreciated by older generations, but the younger population tends to prefer simple and sometimes artificial odors over the complex flowery scents. So, the designer must define the target audience then release the experience at specific points. However, keep in mind, even those that appreciate a smell will grow tired of it over time.

We can describe smell with a few variables. These include, complexity – how many chemicals is it composed of, volume or amplitude – how much of this scent is in the space, qualitative value – what does the scent mean and to whom, and finally, frequency – is this a smell that occurs once a day, or is it something that you only smell in a certain season?

Smell should be used sparingly. A scent, even a pleasant one, can be overpowering with too much exposure. As always, start with none, then add smell lightly and build up. If the scent is persistent, it should be muted and low. If the scent is localized, then care should be taken to ensure the smell is strong enough to be experienced but not too strong as to be sensed throughout a space. If the designer is cautious, it is possible to have many scents in a space, and with practice, it is possible to combine multiple scents across a space to create a sort of chord. Again, smell is the sensing of a combination of chemicals, and it can be like magic, combining multiple scents to create something new.

For smell, designers can play with the simple scent itself, but they are encouraged to explore meaning and memory in the chosen odors. Doing this will unlock more than an aesthetic experience, it will allow a psychological journey based on perceptions and understanding. This may require the designer to research the user's history, but also the user's culture. Are there smells that are pleasant to some but disagreeable for others? Of course, and knowing what these are will allow the designer to avoid a false step in the design process, as well as the exposition.

To showcase smell, we need to use a variety of techniques, but in each, the scent is not extremely long lasting. The reason for this is that smells fade way or are composed of volatile chemicals that decay over time. As time progresses, a scent diminishes. So, useful materials for providing smell experience include perfumes, applicators, naturally occurring aromas, and manmade aromas, such as baked goods. However, these smells must be replaced or replenished throughout the length of the exposition.

Scent can be broken into chemical type, amount present, and extent experienced. Furthermore, the smells can be classified qualitatively by level of satisfaction, cultural meaning, and memory. There may be other ways to classify scents, but using all six of these provides hundreds of variations just with one or two scents.

Smell is a strong tool for design because it is so tightly wound with our psychology. It could very easily be the first sense biologically as it is working with the raw chemicals, no interpretation or structure needs to be applied to allow it to convey information. Because of this, smell can hit like a sledgehammer and provide experience or recall of memories to change the state of mind of the user. Furthermore, we are able to create memories with specific scents through repetition of experience and associating information or meaning with these repeated trials.

The types of smells are determined by the combinations of the chemicals sensed by our many receptors. The more receptors we have, the more smells that are possible, because we not only understand scent from the triggering of one receptor, but also with the combination of multiple receptors. We cannot say there are an infinite number of smells, but there are certainly millions of combinations. Each combination can hold its own understanding, so there is an entire language that can be conveyed just through smell. The question is: how many people are able to understand this language, and how does it change from person to person or location to location?

There are two methods of smell: passive reception and active communication. We use the passive form to understand the world around us. So many things provide a scent, and our evolution and biology allow us to understand many of these, and our experience allows even more. However, active communication allows us to tell the world our stance. This can be a very basic form such as through pheromones, or they can be through the use of detergents and perfumes. How do you show someone you care? Do you clean up for them? Do you bring flowers or food? All of these have scents, and these scents mean something.

If used carefully, smell is a wonderful addition to the experience of the senses. To rely on only the visual is banal, and a quick hit of aroma can enliven a design, or a consistent, subtle perfume can put our minds at ease.

To use smell for design, we need to analyze what ambient smells are in the space, limit those odors that are not pleasant nor are able to augment the design intentions, then we need to determine what scents are appropriate for the design, and finally develop how the smells are imparted. In a basic way, we can partake of smell through our nose, through our mouth, and also in conjunction with taste. In fact, much of the taste experience is actually smell. As we determine the scents to use, we need to employ our strategy of starting from nothing and building up. Again, smell can pervade space, and it can annoy some much more than a visual or aural stimulus if overused and continuous.

Smell can improve a design by scents' connotations and the simple odor produced. We can stimulate the user by providing positive and negative smells, which will affect mindset. However, if we can research or understand the user, we can use smells that affect the user emotionally through memory and familiarity. This is not crucial, but to have scents that have personal meaning can really propel a design in the mind of the user. Because it is so tied into our brain with memory, we can create much more of an impact with it, compared to other senses, if used properly. To use it properly, we must be subtle and with intention.

If we create a design using only smell, we would have an ever evolving space without orientation, and those scents would pass and fade, because of degradation and size of the compounds. We cannot use smell for spatial definition other than general boundaries, and instead, we would use it to affect the point of view or outlook of the user. Although this is an interesting experiential possibility, it may not be a good choice for day to day use, without the other senses. However, there is no reason not to use it in conjunction with the other senses.

If we were to not incorporate smell in design, we would likely have a very flat experience. Although most traditional design does not think about scent in relation to the project, there are scents relative to materials and it is crucial to create a more rounded experience, even if the smells are coincidental and unrelated to the design intent. However, opening our design process to the sense allows us to have direction and strategy to have a more cohesive design. To be without smell, we would have a much more uninteresting installation.

Beyond the typical use of smell, we can use it as an alarm or notification. It could be much more enjoyable to understand it is time to wake up through the odor of coffee or magnolia than a buzzing alarm. We can also use scent as a marker so that one can find one's way around a complex space. For example, we can have a cleaning product or an air freshener that smells like jasmine in one area of a hospital, thyme in another, and other similar scents by department and floor so as to give the user an understanding of place. Again, we cannot orient with scent in a single space, because it broadcasts throughout a certain area, but because it travels through a given space, we can mark each of these spaces with their own scent. Furthermore, it is possible to have scents match or align by floor, to intuit the level of building.

We can also use smell as part of a retrofit or renovation of a space. Simple changes in cleaners, furniture, and textiles, or other items that accept and hold scent, can change the mood of a space. This should be done with a purpose in mind. Although many choose the items to include in a space by availability, these really affect the spatial experience. Can we have an objective when selecting these elements, beyond the visual or the pragmatic? The more we do, the more cohesive the design is. Where possible, we should design to the highest and best use.

There are many methods and technologies we can use to provide a scent sensory experience, and the designer should not ignore smell as part of the design. Although it might be difficult in the current design field to envision the use of smell, with the use of electronics, actuators, and traditional methods, we can provide the richer experience that the phenomenon of smell and memory affords. Out of all of the senses, smell is one of the most successful in integration with technology, especially deploying perfumes with servos and hardware such as Arduino.

Smell Precedents

Food and drink for sustenance.

Perfume.

Cleaning agents.

Air freshener.

Food additives – aromatic.

Draw animals inward, for a purpose (flowers, etc.).

Repulse animals and individuals away (waste, skunk).

Pheromones.

Deodorants.

Define and indicate chemical composition.

Smell Possibilities

Augment and underline emotions.

Map information from another sense.

Communicate / Conversation.

Define emotion.

Pleasure and entertainment.

Mask another scent.

Divert attention from other sense.

Agitate individual.

Reminder or memory.

Wayfinding.

Smell Sensors

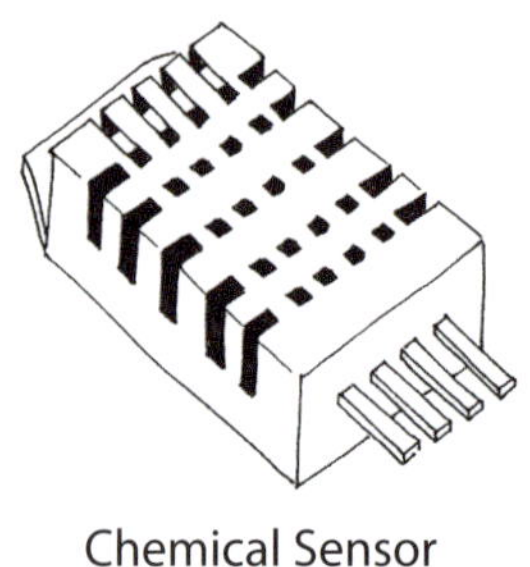

Chemical Sensor

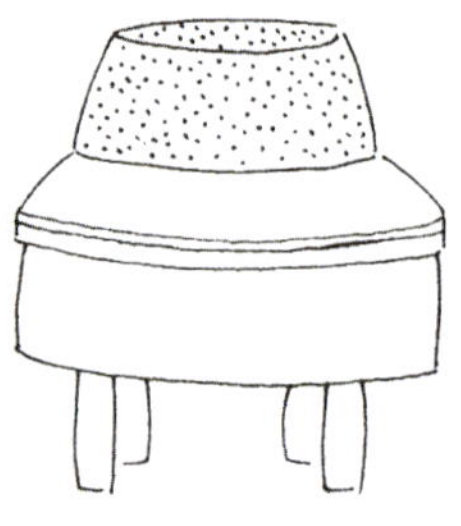

Chemical Sensor

Smell Actuators

Various Modes of Scent

Smell Interpretations

vinegar
dust
heat
wood
smoke

angry

moss
fish
earth
citrus
waste

anxious

woods
moss
grass
basil
amber

confident

oranges
nutmeg
earth
flowers
concrete

determined

floral
citrus
grass
water
berries

happy

water
sandalwood
grass
cucumber
floral

meditative

lilac
buckeye
leather
smoke
metal

perplexed

toast
moist soil
strawberry
celery
mown grass

withdrawn

Taste

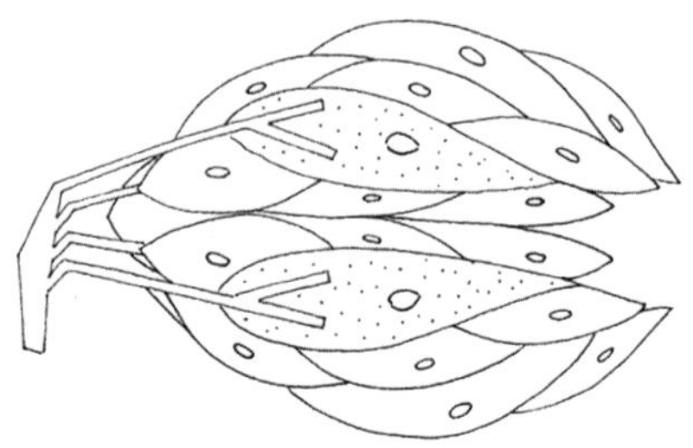

Taste Bud

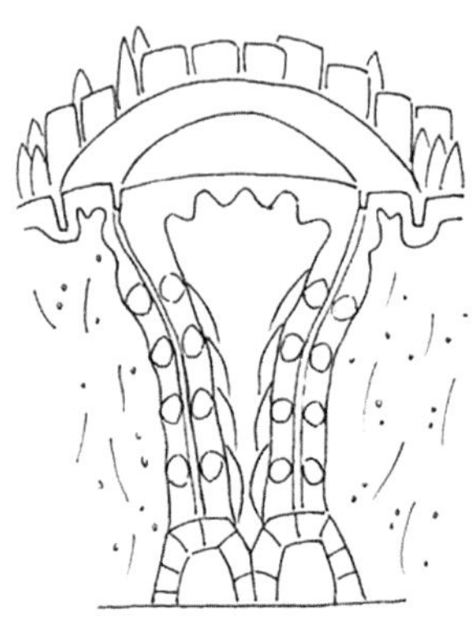

Bud Section

The taste buds are sensory structures that are located on the tongue. These are responsible for detecting the five basic tastes: sweet, sour, salty, bitter, and umami (savory). When we eat or drink something, molecules from the food or drink dissolve and come into contact with the taste buds. The taste buds send signals to the brain that are interpreted as a sensation of taste. Each taste bud contains a number of specialized cells called gustatory cells, and these are sensitive to the different tastes. The brain uses the combinations of tastes from these cells, as well asthe scent, to determine the overall flavor of a food or drink. The interaction of the sense receptors is similar to that of smell. In fact, aroma is often confused with taste while eating.

In order to explore the sense of taste we must place items in our mouths, and for this reason, taste is likely the least important for architecture. However, it is not completely unimportant, and we can use taste to accentuate the other sense elements in a design. The one program that has taste as the main sense is the restaurant. A well-designed restaurant will be designed around the food, and with this use, all the other senses support taste. However, this is one of the few programs where this is the case.

We taste for the enjoyment of food, but we also use this sense to understand the composition of the item being eaten. This is similar to the way we use smell, where the sense experience itself defines the item in focus. This is helpful to develop a knowledge and understanding of what is unhealthy or fatal for us to eat; we develop memories of flavors and we associate feelings and descriptions to each of these. In addition, there are certain flavors that we come upon or develop a negative connotation with naturally–these flavors taste bad without any previous experience.

We use taste when we put items in our mouths, there are a limited number of ways to understand this experience, and there are a myriad flavors, given the combination of the five taste types. Although we think of food and drink first when looking at taste, we can also experience things without ingesting them. This is a questionable way to analyze objects and is not encouraged unless you have knowledge of the item's composition.

Unlike other senses such as vision, hearing, and smell, taste cannot be experienced over distance. In this way, it is similar to touch. Therefore, we need to be near items to taste them. This can be accommodated by placing the food, drink, or other item at the location to be experienced and coordinate how the other senses interact or not at the location. When we use multiple senses, smell is a natural pairing with taste, but so is touch, especially because we must have proximity with an object to use both of these senses.

Like all of the other senses, taste can provide variation in experience. It does this by varying the salt, sweet, bitter, sour, and umami profiles to create many flavors. By defining and separating these taste types, we can draw direct relationships with other sense characteristics, such as color per taste type, where salt could be blue and umami could be purple. But, how do we make these associations? Again, it is likely that any sort of correspondence would be via repetition of exposure or cultural preferences, and in this way it is very important for the designer to understand the cultural context of the design implementation.

Most likely, we should not use taste in all design cases, but it can be used as a surprise or moment of delight. And, it can be used in specific programs as given above or with other senses. When using taste, we will always have at least one other sense, which is touch, because we must touch to taste. However, other senses that pair well are smell and vision. But, what about hearing? How can we use hearing in relation to taste? This can create some very novel and creative designs, and we should not discount this.

However, there are times we should not use taste. First, not everything should be tasted, and what is should be well-defined. Furthermore, certain programs and events should not incorporate the sense. Solemn places, such as funerary services, would not be a good location for taste, but where the grieving gather afterwards could be an excellent place. The use of the senses reinforces culture, and taste is arguably the most important in terms of culture. Ownership of foods, drink, and cooking methods helps build cultural identity. In this way, the designer should think about the group, but also how to bridge between cultures through food, and therefore taste. Defining the similar or complementary tastes between cultures can bring them together, as food is the most basic and necessary element for human survival.

Taste should be used sparingly and with specific intent, unless the design purpose is a gathering or restaurant. As mentioned above, taste is aligned with smell and touch, and without these the experience of flavor is much diminished. Therefore, it can be a quick and natural step to include these when designing a sensory experience with taste. For spaces that are for a social gathering or a restaurant, the strategy should be for the designer to use all senses to support the edible or potable program.

People are not likely to put a random object in their mouths, especially anything that is not food or drink, so the designer must create a space of trust, where the visitor is willing to consume the item intended. Once the environment is trustworthy, we must ensure the food or drink aligns with the purpose. After meeting this, we must consider how much will be consumed by the individual. Is the objective to fill the stomach, like a feast? Or, is the taste experience secondary to another meaning or sensory stimulus?

The best approach to using taste is to define whether taste is primary, secondary, or tertiary, and then select what is tasted. If the item to be consumed is meant as a secondary or tertiary sense, then what does the taste support? If the taste is a primary stimulus, then what senses support that taste? Of course, taste uses smell and touch for a full experience of flavor, but how do we use vision and hearing in relation to taste? Can a sound or graphic describe taste beyond representation of the taste types, such as salt, sweet, bitter, etc. or the literal imagery or sound of what is being consumed? How does hearing affect taste? It often does not, but how could it?

The use of other senses with taste should be complementary, but it can also contrast for dissonant or harsh combinations. Design might not be used to make things better – maybe design can be used to make things worse. If this is the case, it needs to be very clear why something is not comfortable, especially when design is meant to help make things better for people. Using poor flavors and taste experiences, we can sway people, but continued exposure to this method will drive the user away, creating an undesirable installation.

The traditional parts of taste are salt, sweet, sour, bitter, and umami, and the combination of these creates specific signatures. These signatures are paired with the scent of the item consumed, to create flavor, and the sense of touch within the mouth helps define the overall experience of tasting. Unlike with other senses, it is difficult to limit the flavor of an object, then build up. Instead, items will provide some defined flavor but can vary with the amount of elements that create the saltiness, sweetness, sourness, bitterness, and umami flavor. However, the intrinsic flavor, no matter how small, is native to the object eaten, so the designer must either choose the food or drink to work with the tableau, or vice versa, choose the tableau to work with the food or drink.

Because of the combinations of the types of taste there are nearly countless tastes, and it can be subjective to select a taste to match a sensory design experience. Is it possible to be objective? Maybe we can measure the extent of each of the five types, then we can measure on a numeric scale how the use of those align with the design intent. This is still relatively qualitative, but it is backing the experiential quality with a value, and this can be helpful for the designer and user. However, we must remember that the experience is subjective and will vary from person to person.

When providing a taste experience, many will provide a palate cleanser. This is good when trying to provide the shock of the new or separate the next experience from all others. This is a good way to deaden the sense, then build it up, but relative to the food or drink consumed. Otherwise, like many restaurants, you can add flavors concurrently or over time to create a new and evolving sensation. We can use taste to add to other sense inputs to create an experience. This flavor can contrast to the other senses, but it is probably better to have the various senses align and be comparable.

Using taste for design can be considered a gimmick, if done poorly. However, the designer should incorporate taste carefully to create an experience beyond the normative visual project. We might use the other senses more often, but taste, like smell, can pull memory and understanding forth with barely any effort. In this way, it is a powerful sense.

In order to use the sense of taste in design, we must not only define what the design intent is and the taste to experience, but we must also decide through which vehicle the taste will be provided. Is this natural food? Or, is it some kind of infusion? Is there any kind of additional processing that is useful or necessary? What are the requirements within the program? Would it be better to use the smell of the item, rather than the taste? Or, use taste rather than rely on smell? Again, what is the focus? Is taste the primary experience, or is it a secondary or less? Does this sense support the others or do the others support it?

The best way to improve the use of taste in design is to actually use the sense. Currently, design focuses on the visual and possibly the aural. The other senses are typically ignored, and taste is very much the case. Of course, part of the problem is the need for proximity and there is quite a bit of intimacy in the taste experience. So, the use of taste will be limited and will not be in every project. Subtlety with taste is likely not an issue, so the typical mode of working by having zero sense experience and building up is not necessary. In fact, if one doesn't want to consume that with taste, that person does not have to do so. This makes it very easy to go all out with flavors.

It is not quite possible to only have taste, because consuming needs at least touch but likely smell in order to occur. However, if we design specifically around taste, the user must need to know where, what, and how to taste in order to make the experience. In this case, we almost definitely require smell to facilitate, because smell is able to broadcast, and the use of this sense can pull the user to the taste experience. This needs to be designed to ensure the user can orient relative to the smell to create a bearing for the experience. But, what happens when we get to the taste use? What is the intention? It would be wise to have the taste match with the context, and this allows us to ask what the taste of nothing is, because without the other senses, the user may perceive nothing as the environment. Can we rely on the low and subtle flavors because there is no additional stimulation from the other senses? Do we go the other way and use strong tastes to create pops of experience in a seeming void?

If design did not include taste, current design would not be affected in most cases, because design does not often account for taste in the development of experiential interaction. We need to incorporate taste more often, but we should not go to the extreme of always including it. So, the use of the sense is never expected.

Are there alternative uses for taste? Can meaning and information be associated with the sense? Yes, but the information conveyed may be cryptic, beyond the meaning of the flavor. Furthermore, are there items that we can taste that are not consumed as food? We have gum, which is chewed, tasted, but not ingested. Are there other things? What do we gain by eating or drinking exotic, non-toxic substances that are not meant as food but have taste, nonetheless? This could succeed as an art installation, but what information can be given through the use of such a strategy? What could we learn from eating things like treated earth or ingestible wood products? Could the consumption of bamboo complement a concrete room? A wood room? Could eating kelp give us the sense of the sea? With a legend or a key, we could define a code that allows us to share a message through the ingestion of food or drink. Sharing this code might be part of the design process.

In order to use taste to create a different design for an existing structure, we can simply provide kiosks or machines with food products, but it could be an exciting challenge to introduce the use of other aromatic foods and other taste experiences at strategic points in the existing building. Is there a taste to accompany us as we ride the escalator or elevator? Are there foods that can calm us in tense situations, such as an electrical storm? What can be eaten while heading down a hallway and while waiting?

Taste Precedents

Food for sustenance.

Drink for sustenance.

Bitterene on medication.

Gum and candy.

Food additives to change / mask taste.

Snack food.

Comfort food.

Condiments, such as hot sauce, mustard, ketchup.

Fillers and emulsifiers.

Description of chemical makeup of objects for classification (chemistry).

Taste Possibilities

Define emotions.

Translate another sense.

Communicate / conversation.

Augment information/emotion from other senses.

Diversion (snacking), entertainment.

Divert attention from something else less pleasant.

Soothe individual (comfort).

Agitate individual (hot, spicy, sour, bitter).

Remind of past event or person.

Move focus away from something missing.

Taste Sensors

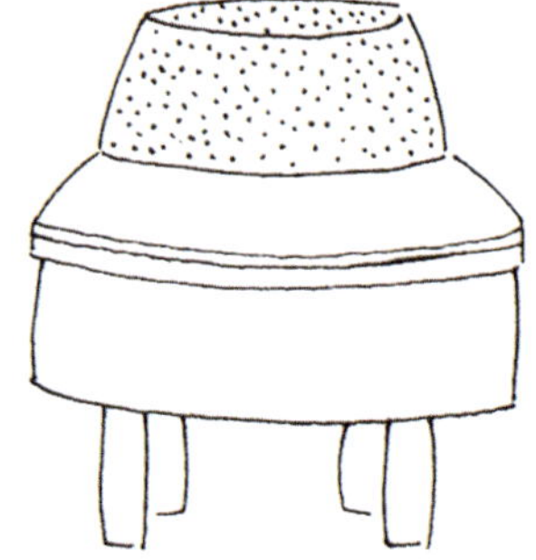

Chemical Sensor

Taste Actuators

Various Forms of Food

Taste Interpretations

bitter
hard
sour
spicy
acidic

angry

sweet
carbonated or acidic
undertones of sour
liquid or sauce
strong aftertaste

anxious

umami
salty
slight bitterness
solid
without sweetness

confident

crisp
fatty
acidic
moderate flavor
aftertaste

determined

subtle taste
floral or vanilla
fat or umami
baked good
acidic notes

happy

fatty
no aftertaste
cucumber or celery
whipped
light consistency

meditative

varying bitterness and sourness
salad
roughly chopped
moments of sweetness
without salt

perplexed

forward sweetness
low sourness
umami
moderate salt
baked or pan fried

withdrawn

Hunger

Hunger is a sense that is triggered by a complex interplay of hormones and other signaling molecules in the body. When the body's energy stores, such as glycogen in the liver, are depleted, the hormone ghrelin is released from the stomach. This hormone travels to the brain and stimulates neurons in the hypothalamus to initiate the sensation of hunger. Besides ghrelin, leptin and like hormones can regulate the sense of hunger by signaling to the brain when the body has enough energy and does not need to eat.

The sense of hunger, similar to thirst, is a physiological response to a need for sustenance. There is an urgency to relieve this experience in order to be well nourished. Although the sensation of hunger is less pronounced than that of thirst, this sense must be accommodated in order to survive. To be hungry is not only about the need for food, but the need for healthy, useful food. One can eat a bag of chips and still feel hungry, because the food lacks nutritional needs. One may feel the sense of hunger even if the stomach is full. Hunger pairs well with the sense of taste, but the designer may very likely use thirst also when designing for hunger.

Although it is not a comfortable feeling, hunger is a very important sense that provides a warning and alarm when we need to eat. Similar to thirst, the sense of hunger may be brought on by influence from others or acknowledgement of fine tasting foods. This is different than true hunger, but the designer can use these other forms of hunger in order to design a project. No one wants to be hungry, and so this is not a sense we seek out. For this reason, we should be very careful when using the sense. However, the introduction of hunger can really make a statement in design, as very few, if any, designers have used it in previous projects.

Nearly any animal has the sense of hunger, and it surely developed through time and evolution to let its host focus on gaining food, instead of whatever other needs and desires were being addressed. In this way, it is a very important sense, because it does not allow the individual to die of starvation, even with the many stimuli harrying that person or animal in the environment. This may seem ridiculous from our perspective because we have the sense, however surely one that does not experience the sense of hunger must be monitored in order to not pass on from lack of food.

We experience hunger when we have not met our nutritional needs. This is likely before or in lieu of a meal, so it is likely we would experience hunger in the morning, midday, and evening, if we follow a typical eating schedule. We might have this sense of hunger after a great deal of exercise, because we have burned so many calories, and we want to gain back what we have lost. Another time is when we see others eating. The external context may either be accidental, happenstance, or it may be because of propaganda and intention. Finally, another reason for hunger is because of poor eating habits, where the individual eats a lot of junk food, or they are lacking some specific nutrients either because of environmental or physiological conditions or because of poor choices.

Hunger can happen anywhere, especially if one of the conditions listed above occurs. However, the sense of hunger is really related to time, rather than to space, at least in most cases. But, hunger is brought on by food availability, access, or nutritional content. In this way, we can argue that hunger is related to location in specific instances.

The sense of hunger is uncomfortable and possibly even painful, and it is experienced on an individual basis. A group will not be hungry all at once, unless they have had the same experience throughout the day, so it is a personal and individual sense that is similar to many of the forms of touch, taste, and thirst. The sense of hunger is not broadcast, like those of smell, sound, and vision. So, there is a clear divide between the personal senses and the shared senses. In addition, hunger has the need or alarm of discomfort, which the forms of touch do not, besides nociception. However, hunger shares the experiential thrill of touch in that the presence of the sense awakens the body to action.

Some may say we should not use the sense of hunger in a design, but hunger brings motivation to find food, and gives the individual an opportunity to partake in eating new or interesting foods that sate the appetite. The designer can set up the conditions and carry the visitor just long enough to be too ravenous to enjoy some food. To ensure the sense is brought about, we can design the environment to burn calories, encourage hunger, or provide a sympathetic response where the visitor sees others eating. Furthermore, the introduction of this sense provides an opportunity to use the sense of taste to satisfy the urge and cravings.

As with the sense of thirst and some of our other senses, hunger is not an enjoyable experience. However, we can use the sense to drive us toward something else, hopefully something of sustenance. When we have hunger we want to not only be sated, but we would also like to explore the sense of taste, at least when we are not starving. In this way, the designer can set up an installation that drives the visitor toward some objective, especially if the destination includes food. We cannot force the visitor to be hungry, but we can help push toward the sense with environmental changes, others with the sense or the desire to enjoy delectable items, some through a form of malnutrition, or with time. The designer should use the sense to urge the visitor toward some object or goal.

In order to drive the visitor, we must set up the environment where comfort may be present, but there is still a wanting. In fact, it would be good for the visitor to not have distractions away from the sense of hunger, which would act as a stand in before the feeling is satisfied. However, we want those visiting the design project to desire to stay at least long enough to fulfill the design intentions, so the space likely should not be solely about hunger and fulfillment. In this way, there is a balance necessary to keep the user in the space while encouraging a sense that is not completely positive. Unlike most of the other senses, it is not suggested that we start with a blank slate and build up the sense, especially because it is innate or existing within the individual. As such, it is up to the designer to determine what is a good pairing with the sense of hunger. As mentioned before, there are several that are top of mind, such as the senses of taste, thirst, and smell. But, we could also pair the sense with vision as it can help induce hunger possibly by viewing imagery of food that is tasty or to evoke an environment that is hungry.

To promote hunger, we need to condition the visitor to have an open mind and be sympathetic to the needs of hunger. This might be through one of the situations listed above or it might be an invitation to spend more time or expend more energy within the design to naturally come to the experience of hunger. In this way, we need a space that can be sustained for long periods of time, and we will also need other items to provoke the sense. These other items are to stimulate the mind and other senses to bring hunger. Some of these include various foods, likely attractive and hopefully with enjoyable aromas. Likewise, we can use perfume, scents, or other forms that provide odor that might be enjoyable, such as the smell of fruit or baked goods. Visuals and imagery are also helpful, and these and the previous items need to have a place within the design project. This could be front and center, like advertisements for food or the condition, or it could be served like a buffet or social gathering. As mentioned with thirst, the design may not be solely about the sense of hunger, and this sense may impel the visitor toward some other portion of the design. Could the food be an objective within the design, hidden and meant to be found? Would it be better to make those experiencing the design to work or wait for the introduction of food, et cetera, instead of releasing it on the front end?

Hunger is an interesting sense because it is very real, but it can also be imagined or brought forth by the mind. In addition, there are different forms of hunger that include lack of any food, lack of food with nutritional value, and a purely imagined or sympathetic desire to be full or fulfilled. So, there is a real hunger for any form of sustenance, a real hunger for nutrition, and imagined hunger, whether brought on by stimuli or through sympathy or desire.

Hunger is a strong solution for design because it is visceral and very real, experienced and extremely hard to be ignored by the user. In addition, the sense can be used with other senses to create a compilation of experience that can act like multiple instruments in an orchestra, and the experience can vary and change, depending on the state of the visitor and the elements themselves.

To use the sense of hunger, the designer should first remove from reach any way to sate the desire to eat. With this, the visitor is tempted and taunted, hopefully quickening the arrival of hunger. The sense is not one of pleasure, and the design does not have to be comfortable, as long as there is no harm and there is a purpose for the discomfort. Furthermore, the designer should provide other sensory cues and plays to heighten the experience. These additional cues can be related to hunger, but they can also be other, varying senses that are complementary to hunger. It is important that the visitor has the experience but is not so displeased that it is necessary to exit the project. How can the designer cause the unease but not push others away? Surely, this is a very delicate balance which will provide a more memorable experience. We might think that the surprise of displeasure adds weight to the impression of the installation. Happiness or contentment is what we usually strive for in design, and what a surprise it would be to convey discomfort. However, to avoid being considered perverse or inconsiderate, the designer must have a very clear intent and use the senses to meet that objective. For this reason, the design should be well thought out, drawn and reviewed, before any physical part of the design is produced. Doing this will focus the intent and avoid waste, both of material and time.

If a design were only hunger, then the visitor must be coerced into first experiencing such, then thinking about its presence, and finally analyze why this is the case. Because of the novelty of a design exploring the sense of hunger, the visitor might be thrown off first, so the designer must provide some stability or comfort in the discomforting experience of hunger. If the design had no other elements, the mind would go directly to and focus on the effects of the sense of hunger. Surely, the visitor would wonder what the thesis of the design project is, but then the experience would pull the thought and discourse toward an interpretation of the sense event, filling the open space within the void of the lack of knowing. The individual will place meaning on the experience, especially if there is little or no prior knowledge about the project. Finally, with time and a subsiding of the shock or curiosity of the experience, the visitor will likely try to understand why such interpretations were created, linking points and ideas in the use of the sense of hunger. In this way, different forms of knowledge can be achieved by the visitor, simply by focusing on only one sense.

If the design did not incorporate hunger, the visitor would not be surprised at all, since most designs do not explore this sense. So, there would be little gained by highlighting the lack of the sense. This is unlike the absence of other senses, like vision or hearing, because to be without either or both of these, to the average person, would be bizarre and shocking. So, the same effect is not likely to occur with the removal of the sense of hunger.

Using the sense of hunger as an experience can provide a designed unease, but this discomfort can be for the exploration and education about such effects to others in the population and abroad who are not so fortunate to think of hunger as alien. In addition, the sense can also be a proxy, in place of another experience that could be much more discomforting. The experience of hunger could be in lieu of true pain and represent harm or loss of life. What are non-positive experiences or actions that can be shown through the use of hunger?

Using hunger in an existing structure would likely be very similar to using thirst. The designer could use the context and signifiers to induce a sense of hunger while moving through the space, and it would be a stronger relationship if the experience could rise and fade with some rhythm as the visitor works through the space. As with thirst, the designer should mark the specific points in the assembly and match them with the design intent. So, like with any design project, every part should be planned and drawn out to ensure the objectives are met, especially because the senses can be considered qualitative, allowing subjectivity into the experience. As such, if not careful, the design can miss the mark because the sense experiences could be mistranslated.

Hunger Precedents

Things that cause hunger:

Being famished.

Suggestion – others eating.

Drinking certain beverages (alcohol, soda).

Conjunction with drinking.

Advertising.

Passage of time.

Chemicals ingested.

Perceived hunger (smell).

Exercise.

Presence of food.

Hunger Possibilities

Sate hunger.

Build hunger for longing or need.

Communicate idea or information.

Augment other sense, such as smell or taste.

Pain, irritation.

Divert attention from other feeling or sense.

Warn against action, animal, or object.

Encourage eating specific foods.

Curb or coach behavior.

Increase drive / motivation.

Hunger Sensors

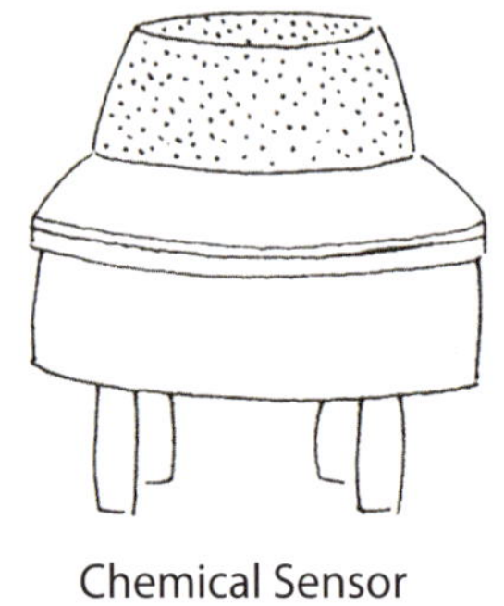

Chemical Sensor

Hunger Actuators

Chemicals and Scents

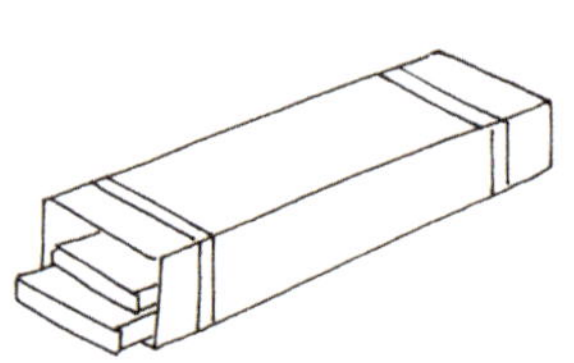

Gum and Flavoring

Various Forms of Food

Hunger Interpretations

angry

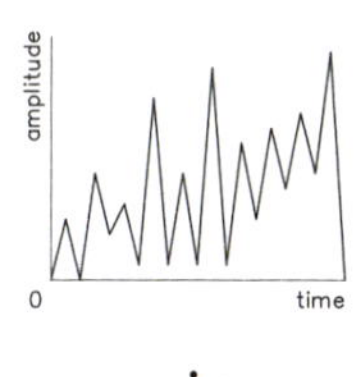

anxious

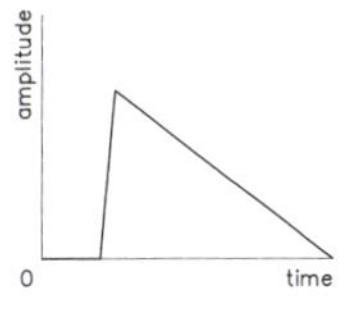

confident

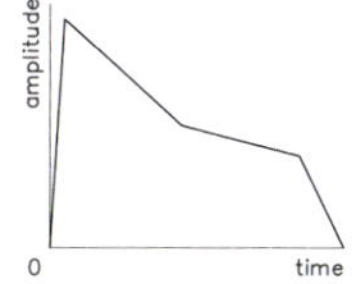

determined

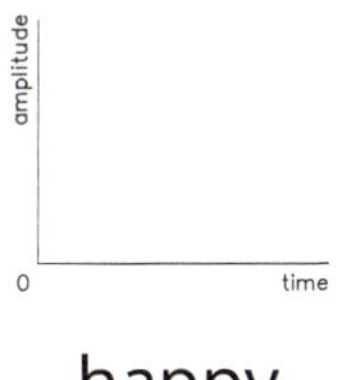

happy

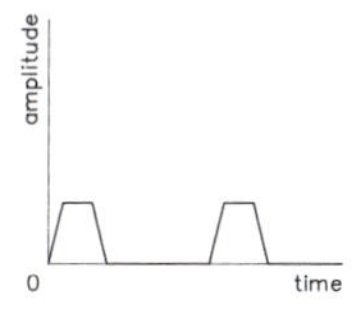

meditative

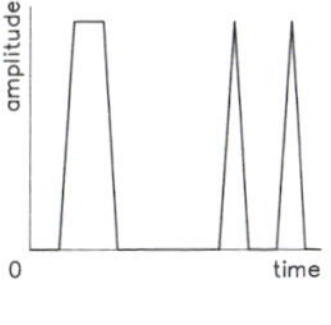

perplexed

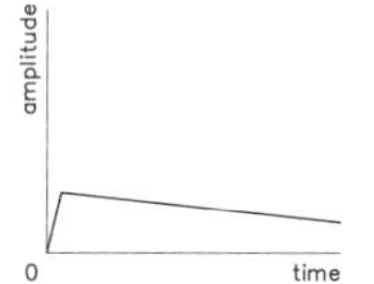

withdrawn

Thirst

Thirst is a physiological sense that is triggered by a decrease in the water levels of the body. When the body's water levels drop, cells in the hypothalamus of the brain called osmoreceptors detect the change and send a signal to initiate the sensation of thirst. In response, we seek out water or other fluids to restore water balance in the body. In addition to osmoreceptors, taste receptors in our mouth detect when fluids are present and help us to perceive thirst and satisfaction of the sense.

Thirst is essential for us to know when to be hydrated. Over time our species has been able to move beyond only the need to drink and provide new options desired or helpful to drink. These include various nonalcoholic drinks, alcoholic drinks, health or vitamin drinks, and medicines. The use of thirst as a sense to convey information, sustenance, and be a vehicle for better health is superior to many other senses because we are able to ingest the substance to be sated or improved. Hunger is similar to thirst in many ways, but its physiological mechanics are different, and though smell affects taste, that sense is not very useful to satisfy the body, instead it is better to warn or report on the chemicals of the items that might be ingested.

Moving beyond the physical requirements forced on us by our environment, humans have had the luxury to explore the senses, including thirst, for pleasure and not just for requirement. This freedom allowed many new ways to utilize our body's natural desires and interests, so we can now use thirst for entertainment and interest without worrying about survival. Although we do not have full control over the experience of thirst, we do have control over what we are willing and able to drink. Water is always great, but now we can drink tea, coffee, juice, alcohol, and other beverages. These new forms of drink provide hydration to some extent, but they also have new substances that please our body.

Again, we don't have full control over when we have thirst, but we can predict its occurrence, and we can even provoke and prod the sense by using forms of encouragement, including others drinking and advertisements. Because nearly all forms of drink are socially acceptable, except alcohol, we can experience the sense of thirst in nearly any situation or location with various liquids. This makes thirst a great sense for the designer to encourage, and because there are so many allowable places for the drinking, the designer can pervade with the desired intent in nearly all locales. As such, thirst is a great sense to explore.

Thirst when experienced with its primary purpose is not necessarily enjoyable and urges the individual to search and imbibe water. The sense in this way is extreme and necessary to sustain life. However, when we are able to have access to sufficient water, we can have lesser forms of thirst. These may seem strong, though they are not comparable to that for one who is truly parched. Instead, the sense of thirst is a motivator to try something that is enjoyable, not just necessary. Though some may think these other forms of thirst are necessary, they are really an opportunity for those making and arguably designing the liquids to provide some purpose or intent. This should be kept in mind when using the sense for a particular application.

Thirst is a very personal, individual sense that relates to the needs of the body. This sense of thirst is different than most other senses because it is not to explore and understand the environment, instead originally, it is to ensure the individual lives and succeeds. In this way, really only the sense of hunger and time are similar. However, there are many other senses that are personal, such as most forms of touch, but they may not have the same urgency as the sense of thirst and hunger. Another sense that can be said to be like thirst and hunger is the sense of smell which augments the experience of drinking and eating, although smell utilizes chemicals that expand in a space. In any case, the designer should use the sense of smell in the exploration of thirst to have a rounder, fuller experience.

As mentioned, thirst can be said to be similar to hunger, touch, and smell, although it is very different than the senses of vision and hearing or sound. Vision can be said to be necessary, but other senses can be used in lieu of it, and it requires a degree of distance and is not a personal sense that can only be sensed by the individual. Furthermore, sound has the same characteristics as vision, although we can hear internal sounds and processes. In any case, we can use the sense of vision and sound to encourage thirst, such as seeing a desirable drink or others ingesting a beverage and hearing the sound of a canned drink being opened or the fizz of a carbonated beverage. In this way, vision and sound are great ways to entice the user in a design installation.

The designer can use the sense of thirst to convey a design intent through the use of beverages and liquids. First, we must understand what the design intent is. Next, we must determine what the use of drink is meant to convey. Is there some chemoreceptive feature of the drink, such as using alcohol? Is the drink meant to complement the other aspects of the design, or is it meant to contrast with the project? Is there some taste or feature, such as color or viscosity, that is meant to augment the design? Next, we must determine how the beverage is presented. Will the design be improved by presenting the drink in a paper cup? Is fine stemware a better solution? Would it be better to place the liquid in a bowl to be ingested either with a spoon or by lifting the bowl to the mouth? Finally, we must define where the drink is located. Is the beverage in clear view, in the center of the space? Is it hidden within a detail of the design installation, and we are pushed to drink either out of curiosity or direction? The designer must be careful answering each of these questions to ensure the use of the sense of thirst is aligned with the intent of the project.

To provide a beverage to quench thirst, the designer should think about how the user takes the drink. Likely, the drink will be presented somewhere between the waistline and eye level. However, what if it is not? What does it mean for the visitor to need to bend over to take the drink or reach high overhead to acquire it? Next, how is the beverage imbibed? Is it taken through a straw? Do we use a cup, a glass, a mug, or another form of container? What if we use a bowl as mentioned above? What does it mean for each of these cases? Of course, drinking through a straw is informal, but what does the container mean?

Not only does the drink need to be presented in a defined container and conveyance, but how that container is presented is also important. Is it sitting on a tray to be ingested? Would it be better to have each drink specially made for the guest? Is the drink sitting in a strange position or location that makes the visitor wonder what the intention and purpose are? Perhaps, the drink containers are presented in their own holders. Would these containers be able to go home with the guests and why? Are they souvenirs or can the holder or container be used for some other purpose. Again, the designer must determine these things and ensure they match the intent of the design.

Thirst can be classified in a few types and each is useful for the designer in different ways. First, there is the sense of thirst to meet the need for hydration. This first type is important because it ensures the visitor is comfortable, without physical needs to be focused upon and instead, the wants can be addressed to attempt to achieve design success. Second, there is the sense of thirst to meet the desire for enjoyment. This second type uses the sense of taste to provide experience for the visitor which can lighten the mood and provide enjoyment. Third, there is the sense of thirst to meet the desire for influenced perspective, such as with alcohol. This third option is to allow the sense of chemoreception to alter the visitor's state and provide a new experience internally and externally through the actions of the guest. Finally, there is the sense of thirst to meet the desire to affect the design. Arguably, each of the other types are leading toward this option in a design installation, however the designer must ensure this purpose is met to convey the design intent.

Engaging the sense of thirst is a strong design solution because it provides a personal experience that can be interpreted by the visitor, but it may also be able to be brought or translated home to provide a memory or echo of the experience at the design installation. Furthermore, the act of drinking makes the visitor the actor in the project, giving tasks to provide experiential variation. Finally, the use of the sense of thirst allows yet another way the designer can push the meaning in a design project. The use of thirst can also be paired with the senses of hunger, smell, and taste to create a gastronomic design experience.

In order to use the sense of thirst, the designer needs to provide an opportunity to drink. This can be a pause in the design project or can be an integral part of the scheme. After the choice of beverage, location, and purpose of the drink is determined, the next requirement is to make it or provide some method to have it made. Is it automatic from a machine? Is it prepared and served en masse? Is it prepared by a bar tender or similar?

In addition to the choices and preparation, the designer should determine if the use of the sense of thirst is complementary to the use of other senses. As mentioned earlier, the senses of taste, hunger, and smell go well with thirst, but what about some other senses? What does it mean to pair thirst with heat thermoception, pressure, or something more asynchronous as vibration, sound, or time? Are there analogs to the sense of thirst in these other senses? If not, how do we pair them? It is possible to create a very complex design with the combination of the senses, especially the more sophisticated combinations.

It is possible to improve the use of the sense of thirst in a design by preparing the visitor with some form of stimulus. This can be any or several senses, besides thirst. Of course, the designer needs to lead the input toward a specific objective which culminates in the sense of thirst and quenched with some form of drink. Or, perhaps the intention is not to fulfill the need to drink, which could be cruel, but it could have some other purpose. Maybe this example would be in order to make the visitor sympathetic toward some condition of another or others. Only after the point is made in such a design would the designer allow the visitor to drink. This could be a very powerful move in a design which would not be forgotten by many who experience it.

If a design were only thirst, the design would be about agony and desire, without requite. There would only be the visitor's mental state to drive the desire to drink from them, and no other sense would be available to take the mind off of the experience. This could be a metaphor for life, or it could be in order to change the condition of the visitor, likely not for the better. However, with conditioning, the visitor could be extremely strong mentally, able to focus and bury inward the need to drink, under the conditions and context. Although this would not be a happy experience, the visitor and designer could learn from such an experience.

If a design did not incorporate thirst, there would be little difference from typical or traditional design, which focuses on the sense of vision, and at times, other senses like hearing and forms of touch. So, the visitor would not be surprised to not experience such, unless told there would be a moment of thirst. In any case, such a precedent would mean that it is important that the designer choose carefully when to use the sense of thirst as to not make it a gimmick and trite. So, thirst would be experienced only once or at most occasionally in a design. Although we are exploring many senses, it is not necessary to use them all at once. Indeed, this is the case with the most used senses, such as vision and hearing, as well.

With the use of actuators and influence, can we use thirst as a proxy for something else which is important or vital, where the sense does not dissipate until the objective is met? Otherwise, the sense can be used as anticipatory or a warning. Although the sense is not necessarily a bad or painful experience, it is not one of joy and comfort, and it can be used as a motivator to push or pull the visitor into another or better state.

The designer can use the sense of thirst to create a different design in an existing structure by coding the meaning of thirst and refreshment and conveying the experience to the visitor as the space is traversed. Again, the use of influence and environmental input can make the sense of taste emerge or wane. So, the designer must define the location of the points of inflection of the sense of thirst and then provide the appropriate stimuli. Then, the motivation to move through the space must be pushed by the designer to ensure the entire experiential sequence is met.

Thirst Precedents

Being parched (dehydration).

Suggestion – others drinking.

Eating dry, sticky, or irritating things (peanut butter, etc.).

Conjunction with eating.

Advertising.

Passage of time.

Chemicals ingested.

Perceived thirst (heat, dry air).

Exercise.

Presence of beverage.

Thirst Possibilities

Sate thirst.

Build thirst for longing or need.

Communicate idea or information.

Augment other sense, such as smell or taste.

Pain, irritation.

Divert attention from other feeling or sense.

Warn against action, animal, or object.

Encourage drinking specific beverages.

Curb or coach behavior.

Increase drive / motivation.

Thirst Sensors

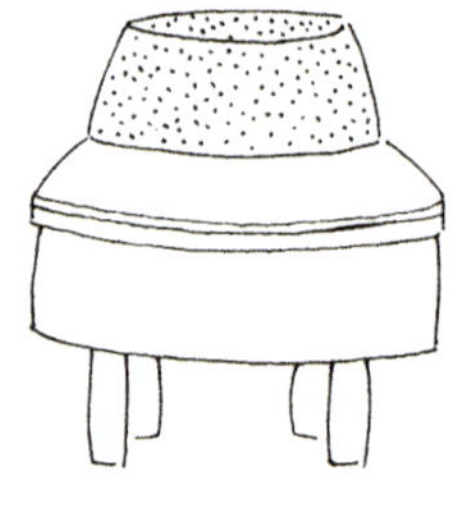

Chemical Sensor

Thirst Actuators

Various Forms of Food

Thirst Interpretations

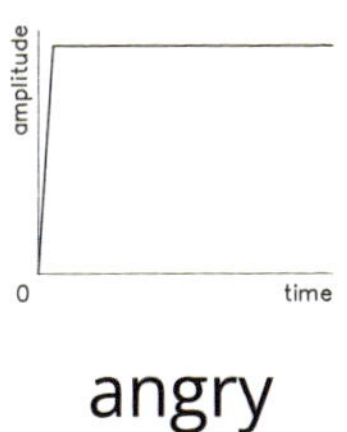

angry

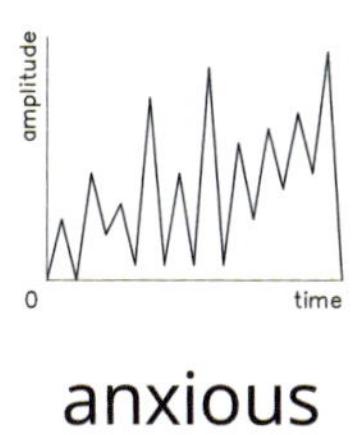

anxious

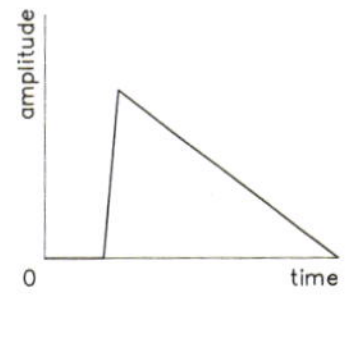

confident

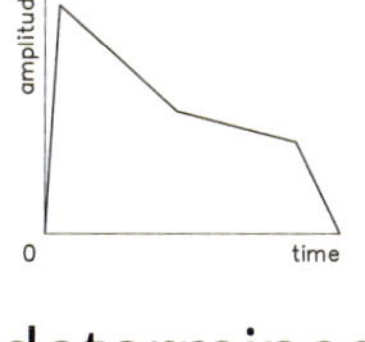

determined

happy

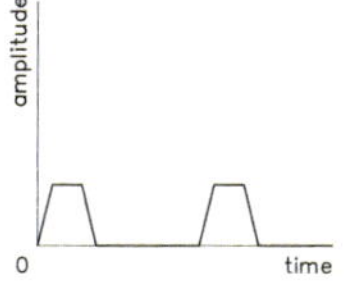

meditative

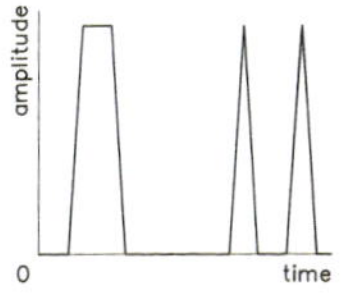

perplexed

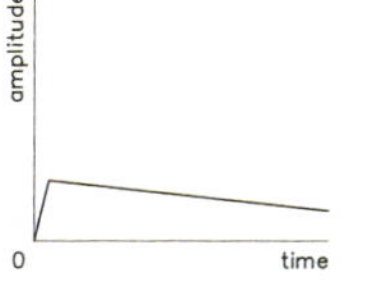

withdrawn

Chemoreception

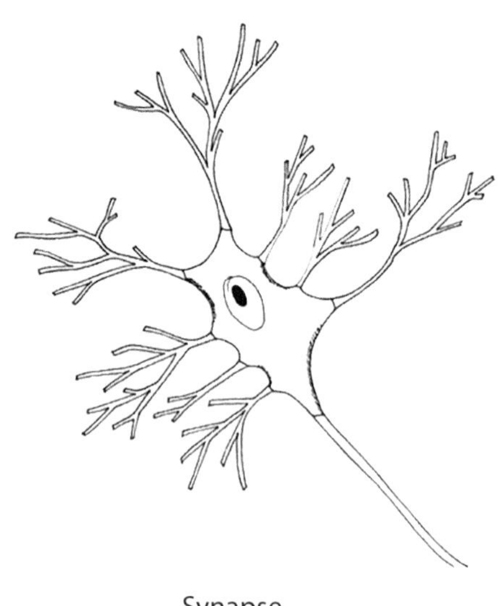

Synapse

The body uses chemoreceptors to sense chemicals. These cells are found in a number of organs and tissues throughout the body, including in our taste buds, nasal passage, and respiratory system. When a chemical substance comes into contact with these cells, it stimulates the cells which send a signal to the brain, and the brain identifies the chemical substance and possibly provide a response. There are several types of chemoreceptors and each is sensitive to different chemicals.

The body is able to feel and experience the chemicals that are placed within, and they can be positive, negative, or neutral. Benign chemicals would include normal or healthy amounts of vitamins and proteins that help the body grow or stay strong, and some chemicals might be able to help the body reach a higher potential. Some of these include stimulants and steroids, however the designer has no business trying to suggest or provide chemicals to change the body and the perception of the world or reality. Instead, these must be personal choices and really should be medically prescribed, as the user could affect the body for better or worse.

As humans, we use chemoreception all the time. Common chemicals that affect us include alcohol and caffeine, and there is an amazing array of other chemicals that affect us through our healthcare providers and pharmacy. These chemicals and medicines can affect the body in such ways as altering blood pressure and heart rate, blocking anxiety, as well as increasing or decreasing endorphins, dopamine, oxytocin, or seratonin. Some of these can drastically improve the way we live and our outlook, but these are not to be considered by the designer, unless approved by a doctor or researcher, and these professions are not likely to coordinate their decisions with designers, as there are ethical concerns, especially when working with humans.

Chemicals can help us and hone our senses, but they can also be very harmful and cloud our understanding and senses. This is why the designer might not be involved with the use of this sense. Some drugs and alcohol can alter perception and could even permanently affect the user. The chemicals can be placed in the body in many different ways, and these include: through the stomach, lungs, nose, ears, and skin – all of these are capable of sensing, and the ingestion of the chemicals can affect those senses or others, or the chemicals can go directly over to the brain to change the way the impulses from the senses are interpreted and acted upon.

The chemicals that we experience can be used or felt in any environment or time, although they should be controlled to avoid unexpected or undesirable effects and changes. The sense of chemoreception is intensely personal and cannot be sensed the same among multiple people that partake in the use of the same chemicals. One can say this is very much like taste or possibly smell, because the sense is local and cannot be provided or sent across space. In this way, chemoreception is not like vision or hearing, but because it is sensed at the body, it is like the other forms of touch, taste and smell. In fact, some might argue that taste and smell are forms of chemoreception, although taste and smell use sensors near the exterior of the body.

The best time to use chemoreception is when all parts of the environment are controlled. There should not be any provocation, manipulation, or requirement to use the chemicals, and it must be entirely in the control and desire of the user. How the chemicals are provided and received can affect outcome, and the user must be calm and confident when choosing the chemical of choice, and the designer should not be a part of this. In contrast, the worst use of chemoreception is when the user is out of control of the body, context, and circumstances. With these beyond the users grasp, anything can happen, and the body can be harmed.

Another way to use chemoreception is to self-regulate the body to create the desired chemicals and effects. We can experience many chemicals because we make forms or similar types of the chemicals in our bodies. In this way, the body can recognize certain compounds and reacts in ways we can understand and control. Surely, we affect our brain chemistry when we react to external events and process our internal feelings, and we can improve our outlook and mindset with exercise. There are other ways to create chemical changes in the body without drugs and other forms of chemicals, and it might be the job of the psychologist or psychiatrist to explore these and not the designer.

Chemoreception is used to change the perception of the individual user and not a group. In addition, the chemical effects will vary from person to person. As such, it is not a very well controlled method of affecting the senses, so this adds to the ethical component that chemoreception is not a great method for the designer to provide a narrative. However, what is interesting is the sense of chemoreception will alter the perspective of the user, sometimes dramatically, depending on the substance. In this way, as a viewer it could be an excellent way to change the experience of the senses. But, it must be understood that there is not a central story or intent, as we have tried to explore with the other senses.

As stated, the designer should not explore chemoreception as a mode to provide a sense experience. However, it may be a moral issue about whether to encourage or allow the individual to explore with the use of chemicals. In a liberal, free space, it would be an interesting variation that would allow a very dynamic installation. However, this is cultural, and many other groups would not be open to such exploration. As such, the offer to allow this should be weighed.

When, how much, and what type of substance to allow in the installation is another problem, since the individual is in control of providing the sense use. Use at the wrong time, of too much, or of the wrong type can create problems with the design intent and chaos or awkward interactions can result. Can we rely on the laws of the local, state, and federal governments to proscribe the substances? Are we at fault if individuals misuse chemicals? Again, it is likely best to not partake in this sense for experiential changes. But, if the sense is used, then there should be a controlled, safe environment for the individuals to interact with the space and installation.

The use of chemoreception can affect the individual in several ways. First, the use of chemicals can alter the way the user experiences the senses. The senses will have a different reaction without a substance than with the substance. Using a chemical might heighten, deaden, or change the senses, and it is crucial that the user keeps this in mind, unless there is a complete loss of control of the experience.

Second, the use of chemicals can alter the way the brain takes in and processes the experience. The user may not remember or remember differently the experience in a previous use. Furthermore, the brain may take the input in a novel way. This will affect the overall experience because it will change the information to be acted upon.

Next, the chemicals can change the way the brain interprets and uses the input. The brain affected by chemicals will create different results from the input than a brain that is without the substance. In this way, the chemical can change the output vastly, and the user may or may not be in control of how the experience is analyzed and evaluated.

Finally, the use of substances can alter the way the body is able to act upon the output from the brain's analysis and interpretation. The body might under- or over-react to the ideas and notions the brain produces, and the results could be extremely different than a body's reaction without the use of chemicals. In this way, there are four ways the use of chemicals can affect the way we experience a space or installation.

The use of chemoreception is not a strong solution for a designer and the designer's intent, however it is extremely strong for the individual to have an altered understanding of reality. In fact, it is possible to not even require a design for the individual to have a new experience.

What other senses are like chemoreception? Nociception, hunger, and thirst are somewhat similar in that they cannot be experienced the same way by others. In addition, the experience of the senses is extremely personal and can only be nearly understood by others through the use of similar chemicals, though the interaction will really be different.

As mentioned earlier, the designer should not use chemoreception to meet the design intent. However, if it were possible to have a safe and consistent reaction to chemicals, it might be appropriate to use the sense. Because each individual is unique, this does not allow the sense. But, the use of chemoreception allows complete virtual transformation of the environment, as the changes occur internally, within the user. This creates an interesting effect that allows elements to remain constant in reality, but vary from person to person.

To improve chemoreception, we must have it acceptable for all in the use with design. This requires care and consistency, and of course, the similarity in response across all of the users. It is not only physiology but cultural acceptance that must be surmounted in order for the use of chemicals. For example, some groups and locations allow the use of alcohol, while others do not. Some places allow marijuana, but most do not. Chemicals and their effects would affect where they were used, while some cultures will not allow any.

If chemoreception is the only sense used in a design, the users and experience would be introverted and would not be shared among each. Therefore, it is an alternate and very different way to look at design, which is usually shared among those that experience the design installation. Design is an extroverted, communal experience, in most cases. To go interior is not necessarily canceling the fact that the experience is designed, but it makes it much harder to share and convey.

Most design does not incorporate chemoreception, though the use of some chemicals may open or inebriate the user, making the visitor more accepting of the design installation. However, this is up to the individual, and may not be allowed in the design space nor within the culture. Because we cannot control the experience and use of chemoreception, we won't allow it, in general. How do we control intake? How do we control experience? Will we be able to do this in other experiential spaces, such as virtual reality or online presence?

Chemoreception is used to affect and alter the body, the mind, and experience. As such, it can be used in many environments, though we must define who has the authority to allow and control the use of the chemicals. Is this something in the realm of the designer – most definitely not. But, is a doctor the best authority? Or, is it better to be within the world of law? A lawyer? But, what if it is a spiritual leader, such as a priest or similar? In any case, it is likely needed that some controlling group has oversight of the use.

Because chemoreception is so individually based, we can use chemoreception with any building. But, the choice of chemical used is an important one. Something that alters perception may not be viable in a complex or deep space. A building with stairs and winding halls might not allow one to use chemistry to affect the experience. However, what is appropriate? What are the types of chemicals and how do they affect experience? Can these be matched with a space? Although this is not proper for design and its research, it is an interesting idea about how we can match chemicals with spaces. This is for someone else to explore.

Although the use of chemoreception in architecture may not be allowed or appropriate, is it alright to think about and discuss, even though it is not going to be reality? What if some groups allow it to be reality? What if some are able to experience and there is an imbalance of architectural and spatial understanding and knowledge. Would we be able to say that those that are open to experience and chemoreception via chemicals might have a deeper and broader understanding of architecture and space? Should we say this, if true?

Chemoreception Precedents

Food.

Drink.

Alcohol and other recreational drugs.

Emotions and reactions.

Medication.

Anesthesia.

Holistic, natural drugs and vitamins.

Caffeine and other stimulants.

Applied products (lotions, salves, balms).

Self-regulating and alteration.

Chemoreception Possibilities

Affect emotion.

Improve mental state (focus, consciousness).

Alter perception (slow, calm, confuse).

Monitor environment.

Monitor self.

Augment other chemicals.

Counter other chemicals.

Diversion.

Stop perception (numb, blind, time loss).

Provide, add, or map emotion or understanding.

Chemoreception Sensors

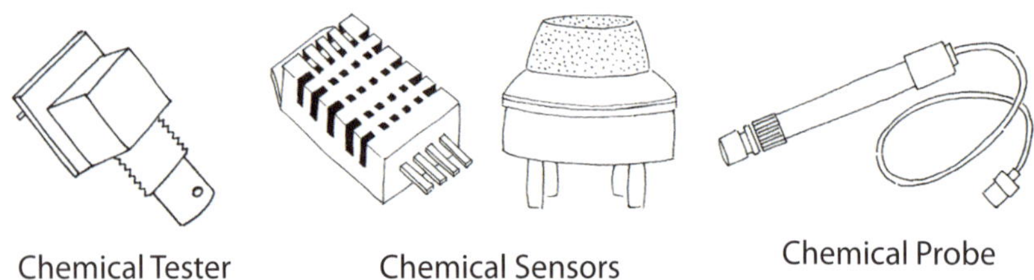

Chemical Tester Chemical Sensors Chemical Probe

Chemoreception Actuators

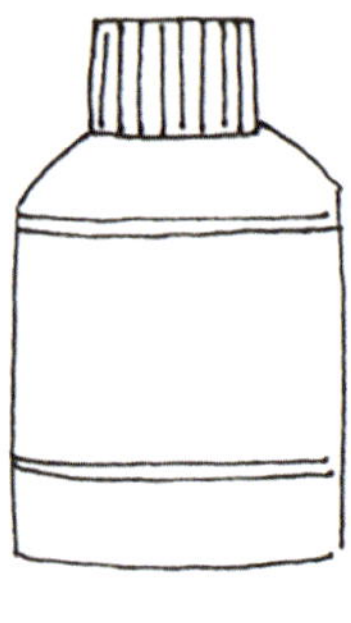

Chemicals

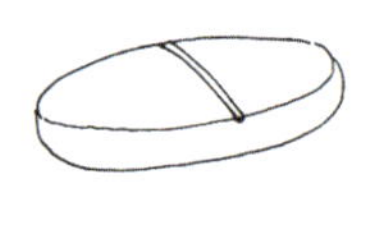

Drugs and Medications

Chemoreception Interpretations

substances that:
depress
raise blood pressure
increase heart rate
allow anxiety
increase metabolism

angry

substances that:
promote tension
increase heart rate
promote thoughtful behavior
increase blood flow
tire

anxious

substances that:
block anxiety
regulate heart beat
increase assertiveness
promote dopamine
promote endorphins

confident

substances that:
promote oxytocin
promote dopamine
block anxiety
regulate blood
pressure

determined

substances that:
increase dopamine
increase seratonin
increase oxytocin
increase endorphins
limit anxiety

happy

substances that:
regulate blood pressure
regulate heart rate
increase seratonin
increase oxytocin
increase endorphins

meditative

substances that:
limit thinking
limit cognition of stimuli
lower attention
raise blood pressure
lower endorphins

perplexed

substances that:
lower oxytocin
lower endorphins
increase passivity
raise inhibition
promote endorphins

withdrawn

Time

We sense the passage of time through a combination of psychological and physiological processes. Physiological processes, such as our beating heart and firing neurons, provide us with a sense of time. In addition, our brain uses some cognitive processes to keep track of the passing of time and to perceive it more accurately.

Using time allows us to index events and actions. Although we cannot control time, we can measure against it, which will give us an understanding of lengths, frequency, and separation between occurrences. By defining lengths of time and times of day, we are able to keep a record of events, which allows us to plan and prepare for future actions and incidents. In this way, we are able to extrapolate from current conditions to understand what may or would happen in the coming hours, days, weeks, months, and years.

The diurnal cycle is a natural marker of time. The location of the sun in the sky shows the passage of time, and its disappearance gives us moments of separation that are discrete. This and our heart beat are our first understanding of time, and by subdividing this time, we are able to create smaller units that are arguably artificial, but that are very useful to provide a record and description of events.

In the contemporary age, we are driven by the clock, but even before the present, we were always relying on time, whether perceived or actual. As we grow, we develop a sense of time that is innate, and for some this is nearly as accurate as a clock. We know when to wake up, we know when to eat, and we know when to sleep. We do not need to rely on a timing device – we are our own timing device. However, we can measure time to understand history and the likely future, and we can measure the frequency and types of events to gather a temporal density of occurrences.

Because time measures the change in space and context, we use time constantly. One would think we cannot have existence without time, as there is no change without it. Whether natural or artificial, we use time to have understanding and control of our environment, and if we are not able to have control, then at least we have witnessed the event and can plan for similar, future events. This perception of an action creates memory which we can recall to help or comfort us. To remember is a sort of log that allows us to grow and learn; time is important for maturation and improvement, as well.

To experience time is to place oneself in an environment and observe and react to the changing conditions. Depending on our mental state, we can experience time accurately, similar to others, or we can have our own interpretation that is heightened by emotions. When we are bored we feel that time will drag on eternally, but when we are enjoying ourselves, time can slip away. Even though actual time is not accelerating or decelerating during these events, our perception shows time as ductile, able to be drawn out or compressed from our view of the world.

The sense of time is both personal and experienced at a distance. We can all follow the changing natural and manmade mechanisms to give us a knowledge of time, but our internal, personal clock can slow or accelerate depending on our mental state and desire to be a part of the surrounding events. In this way, time can be seen as similar to sight and smell, which can sense at different distances.

Time is very different than taste and the forms of touch, in that it does not only operate with personal contact. Arguably, it is an abstract sense, as it is not the use and measure of an object, but the use and measure of the change of an object or objects. Yes, time occurs everywhere, but it may not be easily communicated or conveyed across any experiential distance, and it is only needed to be experienced by an individual or individuals.

The best occasion to use the sense of time is when you are experiencing an emotion or emotional change. Although this can be both positive and negative, the ability to experience shows that we are part of time and that existence is real and concrete. On the other hand, the worst instance to use time is when being part of an experiential swamp or dead zone, such as an empty room.

There are many ways to use time to affect design. First, it is possible to use the sun, celestial objects, or a timepiece to encourage the viewer to think about the passing of time to evoke memories and thoughts about the future. On the other hand, the designer can deny any access to observation of time passing to create a timeless space or limbo. By creating a space that lacks access to the sun, et cetera, a space becomes temporally flat, with all acknowledgement of the passage of time lost or hidden. Alternately, we can use actions and occurrences to encourage the perception of the acceleration of time. On the other hand, limiting any actions or occurrences will perceivably slow time. It could even be possible to orchestrate a space to perceive time has stopped or is infinitely long.

Other ways we can use time in design is to explore and promote time as an aggregation of smaller units, or in opposite, we can suggest time as a smooth, continuous phenomenon. With this manipulation of the perception of time, we might even be able to look to the past and provide the impression of reversing time. How can we use memory and mental phenomena like deja vu to allow this to occur?

We can also manipulate time and our mental state, through work or meditation, to find the zone or groove. This state makes time seem to disappear. Alternately, we can provide multiple systems or schedules at once to create varying states of time which can create complex rhythms and syncopation of perception.

Using time is a very strong solution for design because it provides variation and change just through its presence and its illustration in a space. The morning light is very different than that of the noon sun, and spaces and objects will appear differently. Likewise, repetition or the introduction of a timepiece will create a different experience than letting nothing happen or change within a space.

Time can possibly be classified as natural real, synthetic real, natural perceived, and synthetic perceived. Natural real time is the passing of naturally occurring events in the world, such as the movement of the sun, heartbeats, and seasonal migration. Synthetic real time is the passing of time on manmade timepieces. Natural perceived time is the experienced acceleration or deceleration of time because of events and conditions in the real world, while synthetic perceived is also the experience of speeding up and slowing down of time but because of incidents and context within the realm of the artificial timepiece and the constructed environment.

The measures of time can be classified in multiple ways, also. Time can be measured as points on a continuum. It can also be a point in the future that we proceed towards expectantly. We can also understand time in lengths where conditions are nearly continuous with minimal change followed by shifting states. To add more variables, time can be measured against multiple timepieces with multiple events, or we can introduce the experiential perception of time as given above.

We must explore time in design and seek not only the real meaning, but the perceptual and philosophical meanings of time. By acknowledging the phenomenon, we can change our understanding of the elements and objects of design while also changing our understanding of ourselves and our place in the world. Can the designs themselves change? Of course. Should they change? Surely, the visitor would grow bored with a given design installation without some changes. These changes might be the update of parts of the assembly or the light that hits the work, but the design can also change through the change of the viewer through time. Memory is not continuous, and if we progress through time, aren't we really different people? Aren't the objects in a design perceived differently with time's passage? Time could be a great ally in design.

In order to use time in design, the designer must have elements that can change. Without change, time is perceived as frozen or at least irrelevant. Beyond the elements of change, we must have a method to witness time passing. This could be a clock or natural phenomena. Otherwise, as mentioned earlier, the designer can omit a method of timekeeping to provide perceptual games of experienced time. Furthermore, the lack of changing elements will also alter the perception of time passing. Finally, another entity that can be used to make or alter the sense of time is the space itself. The space can either accept or deny the passing of time through how the phenomenon is placed upon the space.

To improve time in design, the designer must be conscious of the existence and use of time to alter our understanding of an installation or reality itself. Then, the designer must deliberately use time and items that are affected by time. Meanwhile, the installation must work well with the other parts of the design, and the use of time must not be a one-liner while melding with the other senses and sensory inputs. How do these other senses compare and contrast with time? How would the sense of touch work with time? It is an exciting game that the designer can play mixing and matching the senses with time, and ultimately it needs to work well with the the main idea or plot of the design. Without this, the design will lack a thesis or clarity, and each of the parts of the design will be independent and lack cohesion.

If the intended design were only time, then the overall effect would be limited to the continuum of time passing and the viewer. Is time apparent to the viewer? Is the viewer part of the experience of time? How does the presence of time affect the viewer? How does the viewer affect the passing of time? If the design is only time, where is it experienced? What is the space, or is there not a space? If the space is not defined or extant, how is the viewer experiencing this? Is it a virtual or mental exhibit, and how would it be conveyed to the viewer, if so?

If a design did not incorporate time, then the installation would be continuous, without change. In this way, the design would never fall out of fashion and would have persistence in the viewer's experience. Modernism attempts to do this to limit the variation and perception of time by avoiding design elements that rely on or create fads and fashions. Instead, the design is what is necessary and without ornamentation. Would it be possible that decoration and elements of frivolity help define the passing of time? If so, how? Is it the style and method of thought that went into the design and application of these? Does the method change with time, thus the designs change with time? Furthermore, is Modernism actually a fashion, and has this fashion come to an end with new needs in the twenty-first century?

There are alternative uses for time. These include applying time to add texture and measure or mark an event by superimposing time on the object. As such, the new combination or amalgamation of the elements causes a third or other state to emerge. Another use of time would be time for time's sake in that the viewer puts time at the forefront and all thoughts and personal change or development is reflected upon by the viewer, without input or change from other elements or viewers. In this way, the experience of time could be similar or possibly just opposite the idea of the groove or zone that we experience when fully committed to an action or task.

In order to use time on an existing structure, we must either provide or strip away elements that convey time. As mentioned earlier, this could be timepieces, solar or natural cycles, but also, it can be the incorporation of design elements that change over time. These elements might be moveable or interactive features, or they may be the ornamentation itself. Most items of material culture fall in and out of style, and the addition or removal of these can provide the intention of the designer, whether to adjust or simply understand the perception of time. Time is both the index and the indexed, and nothing truly can exist without its presence.

Exploring the use of the sense of time is exciting, and it can be evaluated quantitatively, providing the accuracy of timekeeping or perception versus real, defined time, and it can also be evaluated qualitatively, through written documentation about the experience and feeling occurring through the passage and measure of the time. In both cases, the evaluations can be completed with the use of a clock and a method of recording information and thoughts, such as a computer or pen and paper.

Time Precedents

Universal timeline (Big Bang onward).

Chemical/Radioactive decay.

Solar time (Sun's passage).

Mechanical time (watch, clock).

Using chemical substances to alter perception of time (drugs and alcohol).

Altering/designing environment to stop perception of time passing (casinos, shopping malls).

Engage individuals to lower awareness of time passage (work, diversion).

Remove any stimulation in space to slow time.

Working at others' pace for multiple timelines.

Index time (metronome, stopwatch).

Time Possibilities

Heighten awareness of time passing.

Dull awareness of time passing.

Speed perception of time.

Slow perception of time.

Perceive halting of time (time freezing).

Perceive quantization of time (square wave, iterations, index).

Reverse perception of time.

Nullify time, promote focus (zone, groove, en charrette).

Clarify spatial changes over time.

**Allow two or more timelines at once,
via scheduling / multi-tasking.**

Time Sensors

Analog Clock or Sundial

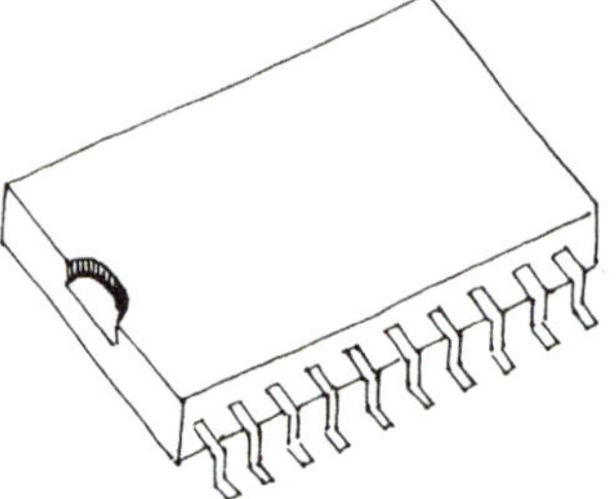

Digital Clock and Timer

Time Actuators

Window

Time Interpretations

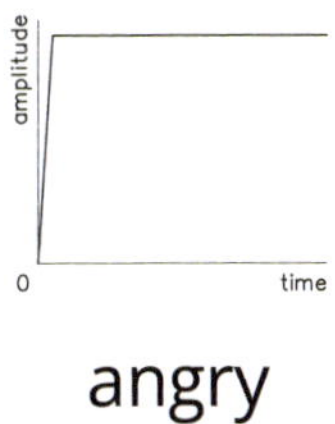

angry

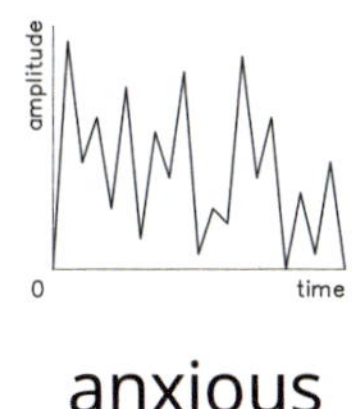

anxious

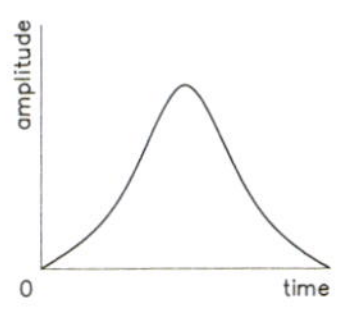

confident

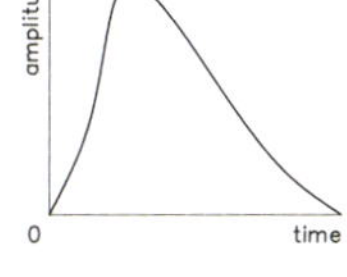

determined

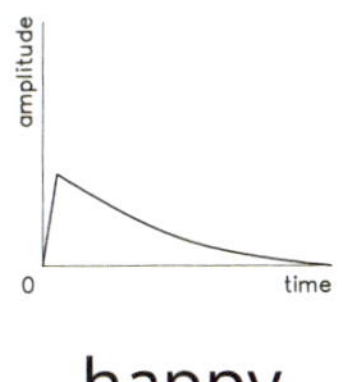

happy

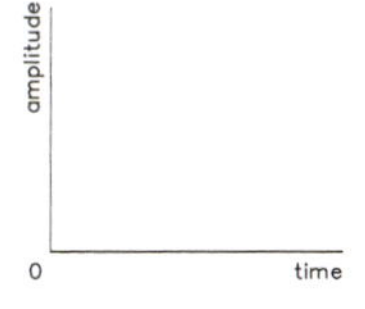

meditative

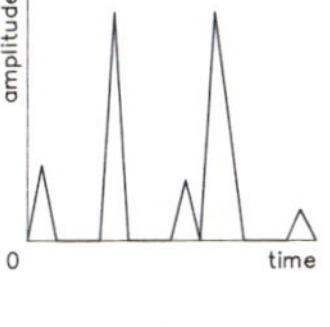

perplexed

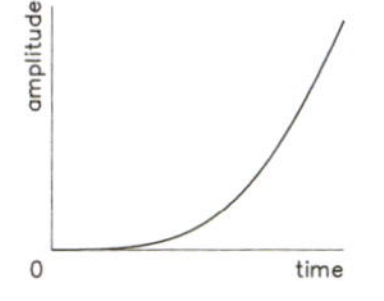

withdrawn

Vision

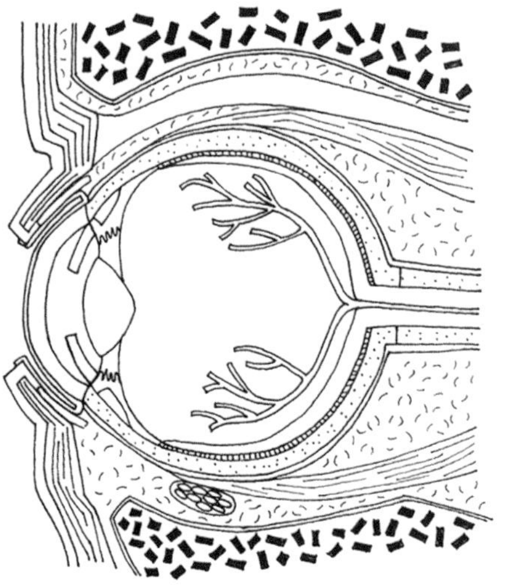

Eye

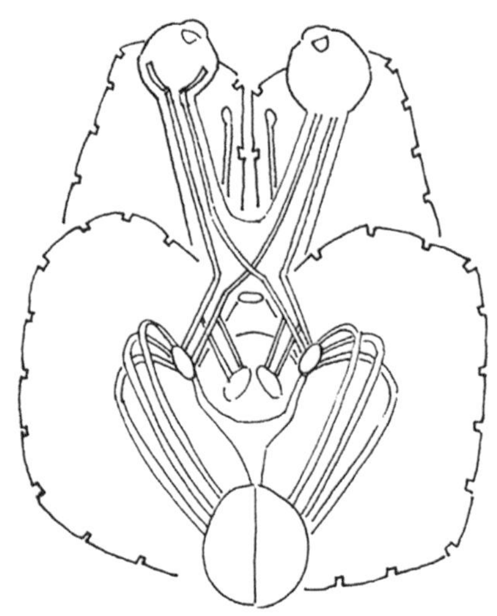

Vision Structure

Our eyes are organs that are sensitive to light. When light enters the eye, it passes through the transparent lens and is focused onto the retina at the back of the eye. The retina contains light sensitive cells called rods and cones, which convert the incoming light into electrical signals. The brain receives these signals through the optic nerve, and the brain resolves these as imagery.

Through our lenses, we receive an upside down image on our retina that is put right-side-up by our brain; this is the first operation that we see, but it is not the only one: in order to interpret the information coming through light, we need to make assumptions and connections with forms and images we have seen before. This interpretation adds to the complexity of vision, in that objectivity may be lost or affected by the understanding and ideas imposed on the signals of light.

Although it may not be the first of our senses to develop through evolution, it is arguably the most important. More of our brain is used to process vision than any other sense. In addition, it is the first sense most people go to in order to understand the world. We use our eyes to see objects, but we also use our eyes to read and interpret language and data, and this sense is used nearly continuously throughout the day. Perhaps vision is not a necessity, but it would be a hindrance for many to lose access to it.

We are able to see things when there is light. This light might be inherent in the object, like a lightbulb or a phone screen, or it may be reflected off of it, like a piece of paper or a brick wall. We are able to capture understanding from the variation of the light – not only are colors important, but variations of shadow are crucial to understand the form and character of objects. When using vision, our eyes collapse the three-dimensional world into two-dimensional projections, so every other variable available to understand the sense is used in order to get a true understanding of that viewed.

We use vision to allow us to passively understand the world, but we also use it in combination with other senses and logic to create, analyze, and evaluate. We can use only other senses, but to see is instantaneous and can be done from afar, without touch and even beyond sound. We can easily see the stars and planets in the sky, but we aren't able to hear or touch these from Earth. So, the sense can work at distance, unlike most other senses.

These qualities of vision are helpful to experience the present and possibilities of the future, but vision is also very important for the past – we use vision to intake information, and we use memory to hold what we have learned. Much of our memory is based around vision, and even though we cannot actually replay the true images in our brain, we are able to imagine and recollect the imagery. Because memory partially relies on vision and our memory changes over time, there are interesting games we can play to explore what our imagination is able to do with the visual information that is used to communicate. We cannot be completely objective, because we have an interpretation for everything that enters or leaves our brain.

Although we use vision constantly, we can use a constructive method of interpretation with sight that allows us to interact with the world to build and change the environment. There is a skill called formal analysis that allows us to understand things through vision by breaking down the imagery or form into constituent parts and understanding what those elements do. Analysis can include the definition of the elements and understanding any actions of these, but also of the shape, direction, and speed of these parts. In this way, we discern meaning relative to our experience and position.

We can try to rely on memory of our vision to interpret, but this ensures the image and meaning change over time, as our memories change over time– we do not hold a continuous snapshot in our head, like a computer. Besides remembering, we can also utilize technologies we have, such as cameras, but also ways to light an object. For example, how does the element appear with infrared vs standard illumination? Ultraviolet? Do we use one light or two, and what is the direction of these lights? How the object is lit allows an understanding of form, as mentioned above. What other optics or sensors can we use to interpret information? Light sensors, infrared distance meters, and laser diffraction are all possible alternate ways to use light.

Vision is both passive and active: physical sensing with the eye and also the processing of the image in the brain. We can affect how people see by playing with how things are viewed and by making associations in the brain. By doing either or a combination of these we are capable of providing new experiences.

Designers can change how people view things physically with light, color, and shadow, as well as the forms and patterns that they see. But, we can also change the experience using optics and effects such as translucency, transparency, and superimposition. With optics we are able to make imagery clearer, fuzzier, bigger, multiply and mirror, and change shape. Lenses and mirrors can make most of these occur, but beyond this, we can also superimpose imagery and introduce effects with opacity and light. Furthermore, the way the imagery is shown can affect the meaning. Images that are projected can come alive in low light areas, and the printed image is a more passive but ever-present object.

In the brain, we can change meaning by association with other elements, as well as techniques such as those used in propaganda. Conjoining multiple elements, creating a tableau, pulls and transforms meanings. To place enjoyed or beloved imagery next to something with a negative connotation will change the meaning for both. To have a positive image next to something neutral very likely will boost the esteem of the object to something that is appreciated. Beyond these methods, vision can be affected through changing the chemistry of the brain.

Vision is a very important and strong sense in our day to day lives. Almost all activities require or rely on sight. Although it is possible to develop without the sense of vision, it could make the experience of some environments and events weaker. Because it is one of our primary senses, people lock to the visual and can perceive information nearly instantaneously. It is not a sense that requires much translation for our minds to get the gist of the meaning. Furthermore, vision allows us to communicate over distance. Light is likely the fastest moving element in our existence, and as long as we have visual access to this, without obstructions, we can communicate efficiently and quickly over long distances.

Vision is used for all of the levels of thinking in our lives. Sight allows us to provide descriptions and remember objects and events. We gather information with our eyes to heighten understanding. We use what we have seen to develop or change something else. Reviewing elements, we are able to analyze how and how well things work. In addition, we look at the results of actions, and we are able to justify content. Finally, we use our sight in combination with our skills at analysis to create new things.

Vision is the primary sense when it comes to most forms of design. Of course, graphic design relies on it, but so do each of the other areas. The immediacy and familiarity make it the first sense. People carry memories of imagery and forms that they can put together to create new meanings. Furthermore, there are similar associations with imagery across a culture, so one is able to tell a story or provide information through an image. Not only are pictures and forms part of vision, but language is as well. It is a code, a system, to provide information, and the letters and numbers that compose the language are in fact derived from pictures. But, when this imagery is viewed as a series that provides information, which can bring about new meanings, we see that vision allows the elevation of form from what is a simple pictogram with a single meaning to something that can nearly describe or provide any or all meaning. Finally, so much of our language is biased toward the sense. Some examples of sayings that push vision include, let's see what happens, look into it, watch out, do a review, and the vision for the product.

Because vision is so relied upon, a good strategy in design is to not address site as the primary sense when experiencing a space or building. There are several other senses to explore instead. Ultimately, we don't need to ignore sight, but initially it could be better to highlight other senses to heighten the phenomenological experience in the built environment. Because vision is arguably the most used sense, the designer should ignore it temporarily and focus on other sensory modes. Then, the designer should slowly, methodically add visual experiences to give a specific idea or tell a story. The architect becomes a curator, pulling senses and trying to communicate certain ideas through those senses. Again, at first: ignore the visual, make sensory interventions, then add vision. This is how we create a better, more experiential design.

To use only vision is what most designers already do. Some might say this is fully explored, and there is nothing left to learn from this. It is important for the design student to learn and explore all the elements of visual design, such as line, color, and pattern, but then it is time to move beyond these rudiments. Instead of going directly to the graphic or visual strategies, define what the purpose or meaning is, then choose the senses.

What happens if we don't use vision at all? What other senses should we use? The question should be, what are we trying to evoke? If we are trying to provide a sense of excitement, we should use sound and touch, in lieu of vision. Of the touch senses, some of the best choices to evoke excitement are pressure, cold thermoception, tension, stretch, vibration and equilibrioception. By using these, the experience could be much greater than relying solely on vision with strong colors, patterns, and linework to provide a sense of excitement. One of the great results of not using sight is the individual cannot see what is about to happen, appearance is not broadcast, instead sensations come out of nowhere.

It is clear that vision is overused, and it could be better to design for the other senses, not including sight. However, what if there are new ways to use vision? What would those be? Can light or color convey emotion, and are these emotions similar among most of the population, or at least, the users? Is blue always sadness? Is red always aggressive? Is it as easy as that? Perhaps, but are there new ways to use sight to affect design? For the sense itself, probably not, but how we use the sense to tell a story or create a mystery or quest for the user through using gamification and teaching strategies is very likely.

We can use vision's design methods in existing structures, as well as new projects. To improve experiential design through sight requires analysis and evaluation of the existing conditions, then we must ask what is the purpose or story we would like to convey? After these have been completed, we can introduce, slowly and carefully, visual cues and information to project the desired meaning. Because vision relies on the reflection of light and color, any form or surface can be updated and designed to help tell the story–it does not only have to be traditional forms of textiles and graphic design. Visual information is and can be on any building element, such as a column, ceiling, floor, or furniture–the location is only limited by the designer's imagination.

So, how do we develop the idea slowly and carefully? After we have the story or design intent worked out, we can determine how we want to convey this visually and on what elements or spaces we would like to place the experience. Then, we remove all visual components, leaving nothing to see or look at–this is the baseline, and then we build up from this. At first, we only explore one visual idea on a space, however after going through this a couple more times, we can build up or diminish the effects or presentation of the visual program. After finding a balance with the sight work, we can evaluate the work, explore other senses, or leave the project alone. It is important not to overstimulate the user with too much visual experience or any other sensory experience.

Vision Precedents

Texture

Line

Shape

Form

Color

Value

Pattern

Rhythm

Proportion

Scale

Balance

Harmony

Space/perspective

Center of interest

Vision Possibilities

Understand physical object.

Translate/map information from other sense.

Abstract modeling and conception.

Augment other sense.

Communicate.

Diversion, entertainment, art.

Image vs. 3D vs. Text / Notation.

Desire, attraction.

Warming, repulsion.

Encourage behavior (color, pattern, shape).

Vision Sensors

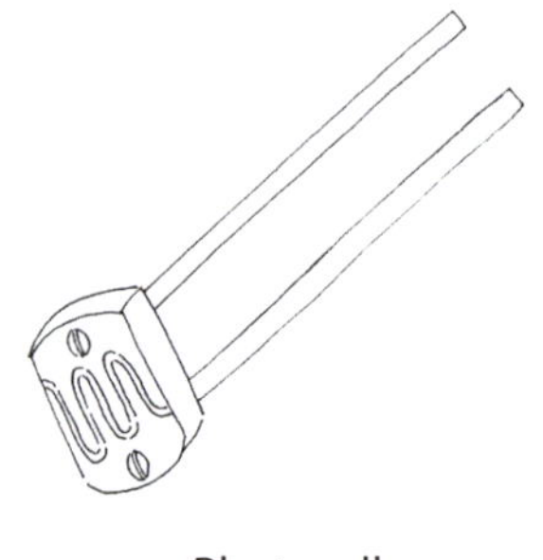

Photocell

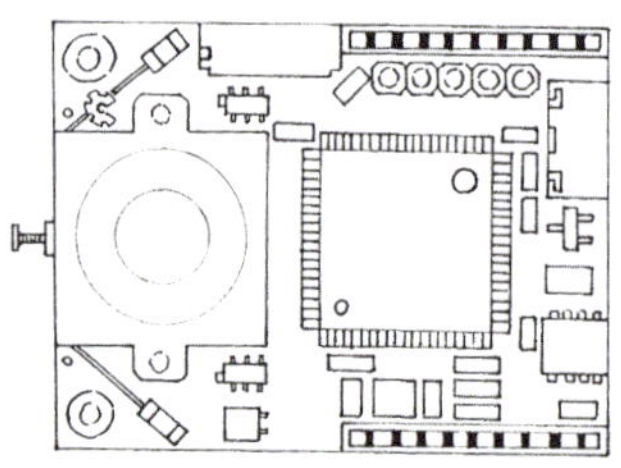

Camera and Sensing Software

Vision Actuators

Elements and Principles of Design

Vision Interpretations

sharp angles
irregular
varying directionality
bold orange, red, or yellow
erratic linework

angry

boldy rhythmic line work
complementary colors
frenetic layout or grouping
rich textures
lack of hierarchy

anxious

high contrast
strong linework
emphasis of subject
minimal texture
strong hierarchy

confident

strong color combination
clear hierarchy
consistent lineweight
bold shapes
use of negative space

determined

matching colors
smooth form and lines
compositional harmony
adequate scale
clear hierarchy

happy

high use of negative space
extensive linework
balanced composition
harmony of forms
singular texture

meditative

erratic lineweight and direction
lack of balance
lack of scale
strong texture
multiple points of emphasis

perplexed

harmony among elements
strong balance
no emphasis
analogous, dark colors
strong negative space

withdrawn

Programming for the Senses

In order to create a richer, more diverse space, designers should stimulate our many senses. The designer already controls form, light, pattern, and color, providing visual stimulation. In addition, architects and designers already make some use of touch and sound: materials provide tactile stimulation and environmental sounds and acoustical stimuli provide aural stimulation, but as mentioned throughout this work, design can go beyond traditional means and methods to use our other senses. In the past, one could not easily express things like excitement or worry through touch, changing market conditions through heat and cold, or provide a description of colors or smells with sound, but with the use of microcontrollers, sensors, and actuators, we can now relate one sense with another in various ways.

Before engaging in a brief survey of programming and the use of electronics, we should ensure we have a design objective to keep us focused on the intent, because the many combinations possible through the use of a microcontroller or similar can obfuscate or draw attention away from the designer's goal, if misused. For inspiration and hints, we can look at the precedents and possibilities given with each of the senses in this work, and then, we can determine the best relationship between that which is sensed and the action.

A microcontroller, such as the Arduino, requires a conditional statement that will allow an action to take place. *If this, then this* creates a cause and effect, and the cause can either be something inherent or measured on the controller, such as time or a random number generator, or through measurements provided by a sensor. For the use of electronics in interiors and architecture, sensors are generally more likely the source for the "cause" part of the conditional statement. Sensors provided earlier in the work are options for this input, though there are other sensors available, as well.

The designer can program the microcontroller with some instruction for action as the "effect," in response to the input given from the sensors. This action may simply be to measure the signal from the sensor, but for our purposes, it is more likely that the instructions will make some change or actions using actuators, displays, or other output devices. Many examples of actuators are provided in the earlier sections on the senses. Because the microcontroller translates the input from the sensor as a number, the output can be mapped from the input levels in various ways. As such, the designer can map or translate information from one sense to another. For example, we can map taste to cold thermoception or hearing to tension. In this way, the designer does not only have a great number of actuators and outputs possible, but there are many ways these can interact with the values of the inputs. These will be explored through simple programs using the Arduino microcontroller in the following pages.

There are many variations of microcontrollers the designer can use, but the Arduino is one of the most popular. In addition, there are many different Arduino boards to suit the designer's needs. For the examples here, any Arduino will do, or it is possible to complete the same actions with one of the many other controllers with the right interface.

Arduino uses the Processing language to create sketches, which are small programs that drive the microcontroller. Here, we will look at five relationships of input and output.

First, the Conditional Statement (If / Then) is one of the most basic actions for the microcontroller. It is simply the response to some input. In addition, we can stack multiple conditional statements to have more specific or more nuanced outputs. These are explored in the following options.

With Binary Mapping (On / Off), we can use the conditional statement to turn something on or off. If X, then 1. This is a simple action, but it is very useful in creating a dynamic environment.

One-to-One mapping treats the input and the output as continua, with some value, usually 0 to 127. The input and output can have either a direct relationship, where the output grows as the input grows, or it can have an indirect relationship, where the output shrinks as the input grows. In either case, one acts proportionately with the other.

When mapping the Threshold, the output will not happen until the input reaches some value. For example, the lights will not turn on until there is a minimum temperature in the room.

Mapping Thresholds adds a level of complexity where several things can happen depending on the level of the input. As an example, the number of tiles that can change color depends on the number of people in a room: one tile for one to nine people, two tiles for ten to fourteen people, three tiles for fifteen to forty-five people, et cetera.

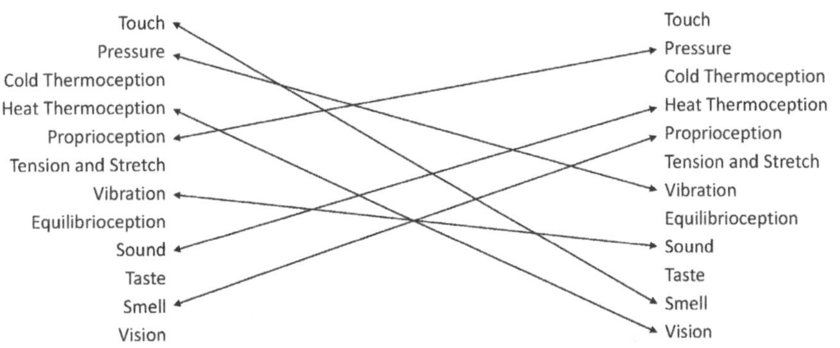
Touch
Pressure
Cold Thermoception
Heat Thermoception
Proprioception
Tension and Stretch
Vibration
Equilibrioception
Sound
Taste
Smell
Vision
Touch
Pressure
Cold Thermoception
Heat Thermoception
Proprioception
Tension and Stretch
Vibration
Equilibrioception
Sound
Taste
Smell
Vision

Conditional Statements

If...Then...

Arduino Example Code to Modify for Use

```
/*
 Conditionals - If statement

 This example demonstrates the use
of if() statements.
 It reads the state of a potentiometer
(an analog input) and turns on an LED
 only if the potentiometer goes above
a certain threshold level. It prints the
 analog value regardless of the level.

 The circuit:
 - potentiometer
   Center pin of the potentiometer
goes to analog pin 0.
   Side pins of the potentiometer go to
+5V and ground.
 - LED connected from digital pin 13
to ground through 220 ohm resistor

 - Note: On most Arduino boards,
there is already an LED on the board
connected
   to pin 13, so you don't need any
extra components for this example.

 created 17 Jan 2009
 modified 9 Apr 2012
 by Tom Igoe

 This example code is in the public
domain.

 https://www.arduino.cc/en/Tutorial/
BuiltInExamples/ifStatementCondi-
tional
*/

// These constants won't change:
const int analogPin = A0;  // pin that
the sensor is attached to
const int ledPin = 13;     // pin that the
LED is attached to
const int threshold = 400; // an arbi-
trary threshold level that's in the range
of the analog input

void setup() {
 // initialize the LED pin as an output:
 pinMode(ledPin, OUTPUT);
 // initialize serial communications:
 Serial.begin(9600);
```

```
}

void loop() {
 // read the value of the potentiom-
eter:
 int analogValue =
analogRead(analogPin);

 // if the analog value is high enough,
turn on the LED:
 if (analogValue > threshold) {
  digitalWrite(ledPin, HIGH);
 } else {
  digitalWrite(ledPin, LOW);
 }

 // print the analog value:
 Serial.println(analogValue);
 delay(1); // delay in between reads
for stability
}
```

Alternate Example Code

```
const int touchSensorPin = 2;
const int buzzerPin = 3;

void setup() {
 pinMode(touchSensorPin, INPUT);
 pinMode(buzzerPin, OUTPUT);
}

void loop() {
 int touchState = digitalRead(touch-
SensorPin);

 if(touchState == HIGH) { // When the
sensor is touched
  tone(buzzerPin, 1000); // Produce a
sound with frequency 1000Hz
  delay(100);          // Sound for 100ms
  noTone(buzzerPin);    // Stop the
sound
 }
}
```

Binary Mapping

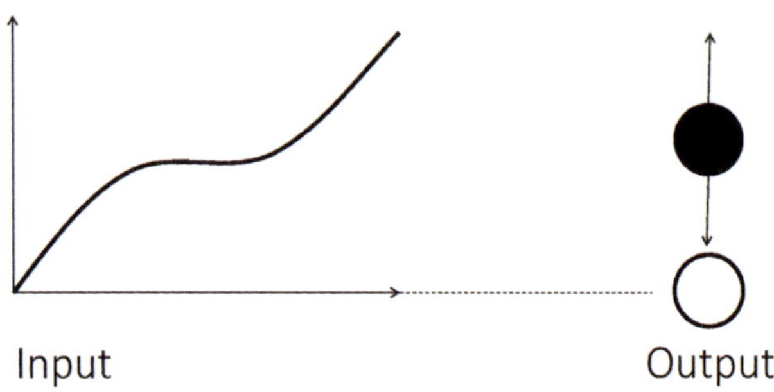

Arduino Example Code to Modify for Use

```
/*
  Analog Input

  Demonstrates analog input by reading an analog sensor on analog pin 0 and
  turning on and off a light emitting diode(LED) connected to digital pin 13.
  The amount of time the LED will be on and off depends on the value obtained
  by analogRead().

  The circuit:
  - potentiometer
    center pin of the potentiometer to the analog input 0
    one side pin (either one) to ground
    the other side pin to +5V
  - LED
    anode (long leg) attached to digital output 13 through 220 ohm resistor
    cathode (short leg) attached to ground

  - Note: because most Arduinos have a built-in LED attached to pin 13 on the
    board, the LED is optional.

  created by David Cuartielles
  modified 30 Aug 2011
  By Tom Igoe

  This example code is in the public domain.

  https://www.arduino.cc/en/Tutorial/BuiltInExamples/AnalogInput
*/

int sensorPin = A0;   // select the input pin for the potentiometer
int ledPin = 13;      // select the pin for the LED
int sensorValue = 0;  // variable to store the value coming from the sensor

void setup() {
  // declare the ledPin as an OUTPUT:
  pinMode(ledPin, OUTPUT);
}
```

```
void loop() {
 // read the value from the sensor:
 sensorValue = analogRead(sensor-
Pin);
 // turn the ledPin on
 digitalWrite(ledPin, HIGH);
 // stop the program for <sensorVal-
ue> milliseconds:
 delay(sensorValue);
 // turn the ledPin off:
 digitalWrite(ledPin, LOW);
 // stop the program for for <sensor-
Value> milliseconds:
 delay(sensorValue);
}
```

Alternate Example Code

```
const int fsrPin = A0;
const int ledPin = 3;
const int threshold = 200; // Adjust as
needed based on your testing

void setup() {
 pinMode(ledPin, OUTPUT);
 Serial.begin(9600); // For debugging
}

void loop() {
 int fsrReading = analogRead(fsrPin);
 Serial.println(fsrReading); // Print FSR
reading to the Serial Monitor

 if (fsrReading > threshold) {
  digitalWrite(ledPin, HIGH); // Turn
on LED if tension is detected
 } else {
  digitalWrite(ledPin, LOW); // Turn
off LED otherwise
 }

 delay(100); // Delay for 100ms
}
```

One-to-One

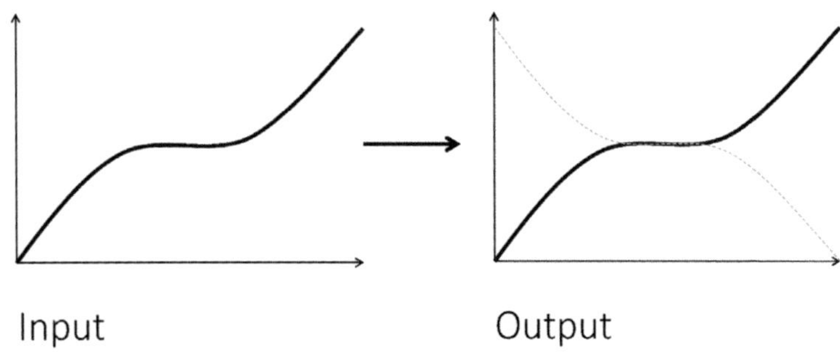

Arduino Example Code to Modify for Use

```
/*
 * MotorKnob
 *
 * A stepper motor follows the turns of a potentiometer
 * (or other sensor) on analog input 0.
 *
 * http://www.arduino.cc/en/Reference/Stepper
 * This example code is in the public domain.
 */

#include <Stepper.h>

// change this to the number of steps on your motor
#define STEPS 100

// create an instance of the stepper class, specifying
// the number of steps of the motor and the pins it's
// attached to
Stepper stepper(STEPS, 8, 9, 10, 11);

// the previous reading from the analog input
int previous = 0;

void setup() {
  // set the speed of the motor to 30 RPMs
  stepper.setSpeed(30);
}

void loop() {
  // get the sensor value
  int val = analogRead(0);

  // move a number of steps equal to the change in the
  // sensor reading
  stepper.step(val - previous);

  // remember the previous value of the sensor
  previous = val;
}
```

Alternate Example Code

```
#include <Wire.h>

const int motorPin = 3;

int16_t ax, ay, az;
float angle;

void setup() {
 Wire.begin();
 Serial.begin(9600);

 // Initialize MPU-6050
 Wire.beginTransmission(0x68);
 Wire.write(0x6B);
 Wire.write(0);
 Wire.endTransmission(true);

 pinMode(motorPin, OUTPUT);
}

void loop() {
 // Read raw accelerometer data
 Wire.beginTransmission(0x68);
 Wire.write(0x3B);
 Wire.endTransmission(false);
 Wire.requestFrom(0x68, 6, true);

 ax = Wire.read() << 8 | Wire.read();
 ay = Wire.read() << 8 | Wire.read();
 az = Wire.read() << 8 | Wire.read();

 // Calculate tilt angle in the X-Y plane
 angle = atan2(ay, ax) * 180 / PI;

 // Convert angle to vibration intensity
(0 to 255)
 int intensity = map(abs(angle), 0, 90,
0, 255);
 analogWrite(motorPin, intensity);

 delay(100); // Delay for 100ms
}
```

Threshold

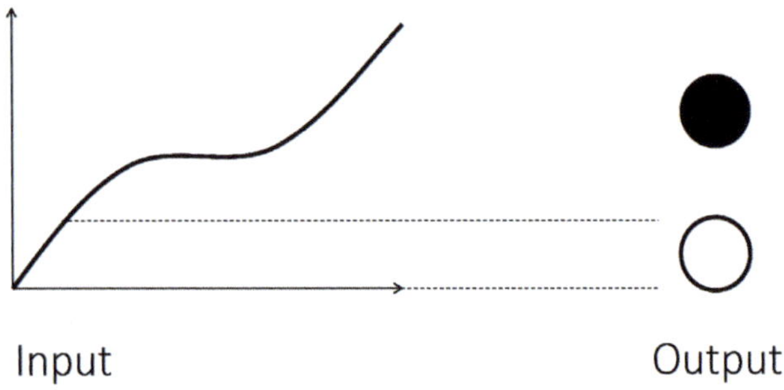

Arduino Example Code to Modify for Use

```
/*
 Knock Sensor

 This sketch reads a piezo element to
detect a knocking sound.
 It reads an analog pin and compares
the result to a set threshold.
 If the result is greater than the thresh-
old, it writes "knock" to the serial
 port, and toggles the LED on pin 13.

 The circuit:
        - positive connection of the
piezo attached to analog in 0
        - negative connection of the
piezo attached to ground
        - 1 megohm resistor at-
tached from analog in 0 to ground

 created 25 Mar 2007
 by David Cuartielles <http://www.0j0.
org>
 modified 30 Aug 2011
 by Tom Igoe

 This example code is in the public
domain.

 https://www.arduino.cc/en/Tutorial/
BuiltInExamples/Knock
*/


// these constants won't change:
const int ledPin = 13;      // LED con-
nected to digital pin 13
const int knockSensor = A0; // the
piezo is connected to analog pin 0
const int threshold = 100;  // thresh-
old value to decide when the detected
sound is a knock or not


// these variables will change:
int sensorReading = 0; // variable to
store the value read from the sensor
pin
int ledState = LOW;    // variable used
to store the last LED status, to toggle
the light

void setup() {
```

```
 pinMode(ledPin, OUTPUT); // declare
the ledPin as as OUTPUT
 Serial.begin(9600);       // use the serial
port
}

void loop() {
 // read the sensor and store it in the
variable sensorReading:
 sensorReading = analogRead(knock-
Sensor);

 // if the sensor reading is greater than
the threshold:
 if (sensorReading >= threshold) {
  // toggle the status of the ledPin:
  ledState = !ledState;
  // update the LED pin itself:
  digitalWrite(ledPin, ledState);
  // send the string "Knock!" back to
the computer, followed by newline
  Serial.println("Knock!");
 }
 delay(100); // delay to avoid over-
loading the serial port buffer
}
```

Alternate Example Code

```
const int lm35Pin = A0; // LM35 con-
nected to analog pin A0
const int motorPin = 3; // Motor con-
trol connected to digital pin 3

float temperature;

void setup() {
 pinMode(motorPin, OUTPUT);
 analogReference(INTERNAL); // For
boards with 3.3V ADC reference (like
Uno)
 Serial.begin(9600);       // For debug-
ging
}

void loop() {
 temperature = readTemperature();
 Serial.print("Temperature: ");
 Serial.println(temperature);

 if (temperature > 95.0) { // if tempera-
ture goes above 95°F
  digitalWrite(motorPin, HIGH); // Turn
on the motor
 } else {
  digitalWrite(motorPin, LOW);  // Turn
off the motor
 }
 delay(1000); // Delay for 1 second
}

float readTemperature() {
 float voltage = analogRead(lm35Pin)
* (5.0 / 1023.0);
 float tempC = voltage * 100.0;
// Convert voltage to temperature in
°C
 float tempF = (tempC * 9.0 / 5.0) +
32.0;       // Convert temperature to °F
 return tempF;
}
```

Thresholds

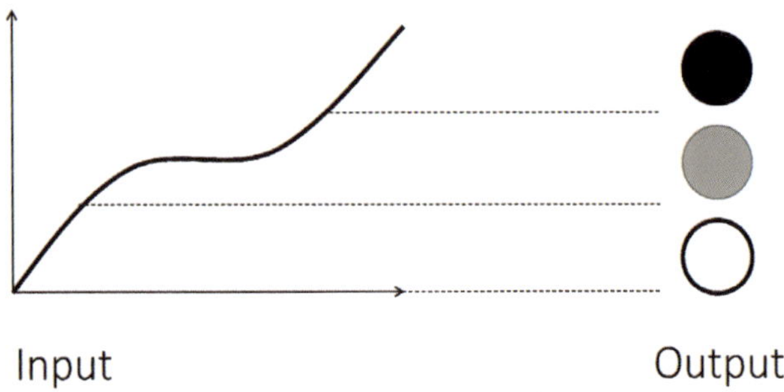

Arduino Example Code to Modify for Use

```
/*
 Arduino Starter Kit example
 Project 3 - Love-O-Meter

 This sketch is written to accompany
Project 3 in the
 Arduino Starter Kit

 Parts required:
 - one TMP36 temperature sensor
 - three red LEDs
 - three 220 ohm resistors

 created 13 Sep 2012
 by Scott Fitzgerald

 https://store.arduino.cc/genuino-start-
er-kit

 This example code is part of the public
domain.
*/

// named constant for the pin the sensor
is connected to
const int sensorPin = A0;
// room temperature in Celsius
const float baselineTemp = 20.0;

void setup() {
 // open a serial connection to display
values
 Serial.begin(9600);
 // set the LED pins as outputs
 // the for() loop saves some extra
coding
 for (int pinNumber = 2; pinNumber < 5;
pinNumber++) {
   pinMode(pinNumber, OUTPUT);
   digitalWrite(pinNumber, LOW);
 }
}

void loop() {
 // read the value on AnalogIn pin 0 and
store it in a variable
 int sensorVal = analogRead(sensorPin);

 // send the 10-bit sensor value out the
serial port
 Serial.print("sensor Value: ");
 Serial.print(sensorVal);

 // convert the ADC reading to voltage
 float voltage = (sensorVal / 1024.0) * 5.0;

 // Send the voltage level out the Serial
port
 Serial.print(", Volts: ");
 Serial.print(voltage);

 // convert the voltage to temperature
in degrees C
 // the sensor changes 10 mV per degree
 // the datasheet says there's a 500 mV
offset
```

```
 // ((voltage - 500 mV) times 100)
 Serial.print(", degrees C: ");
 float temperature = (voltage - .5) * 100;
 Serial.println(temperature);

 // if the current temperature is lower
than the baseline turn off all LEDs
 if (temperature < baselineTemp + 2) {
  digitalWrite(2, LOW);
  digitalWrite(3, LOW);
  digitalWrite(4, LOW);
 } // if the temperature rises 2-4 degrees,
turn an LED on
 else if (temperature >= baselineTemp +
2 && temperature < baselineTemp + 4) {
  digitalWrite(2, HIGH);
  digitalWrite(3, LOW);
  digitalWrite(4, LOW);
 } // if the temperature rises 4-6 degrees,
turn a second LED on
 else if (temperature >= baselineTemp +
4 && temperature < baselineTemp + 6) {
  digitalWrite(2, HIGH);
  digitalWrite(3, HIGH);
  digitalWrite(4, LOW);
 } // if the temperature rises more than 6
degrees, turn all LEDs on
 else if (temperature >= baselineTemp
+ 6) {
  digitalWrite(2, HIGH);
  digitalWrite(3, HIGH);
  digitalWrite(4, HIGH);
 }
 delay(1);
}
```

Alternate Example Code

```
#include <Servo.h>
#include "arduinoFFT.h"

#define SAMPLES 128          // Amount
of samples for FFT. Increase for more
precision but slower performance.
#define SAMPLING_FREQUENCY 2000 //
Sampling frequency of the microphone.

Servo servo1;
Servo servo2;

unsigned int sampling_period_us;
unsigned long microseconds;

double vReal[SAMPLES];
double vImag[SAMPLES];

arduinoFFT FFT = arduinoFFT();

void setup() {
 Serial.begin(115200);

 servo1.attach(9);
 servo2.attach(10);

 servo1.write(0);
 servo2.write(0);

 sampling_period_us = round(1000000
* (1.0 / SAMPLING_FREQUENCY));
}

void loop() {
 /* Acquiring data */
 for (int i = 0; i < SAMPLES; i++) {
  vReal[i] = analogRead(A0); // Read
microphone
  vImag[i] = 0;
  delayMicroseconds(sampling_peri-
od_us);
 }

 /* Processing data */
 FFT.Windowing(vReal, SAMPLES, FFT_
WIN_TYP_HAMMING, FFT_FORWARD);
 FFT.Compute(vReal, vImag, SAMPLES,
FFT_FORWARD);
 FFT.ComplexToMagnitude(vReal,
vImag, SAMPLES);

 double peak = FFT.MajorPeak(vReal,
SAMPLES, SAMPLING_FREQUENCY);

 /* Control servos based on sound
frequency */
 if (peak > 1000 && peak < 10000) {
  servo1.write(90);
  delay(1000); // Delay to give servo
time to turn
  servo1.write(0);
 } else if (peak > 10000) {
  servo2.write(90);
  delay(1000);
  servo2.write(0);
 }
 delay(1000); // Wait a bit before next
sample
}
```

Resources

GENERAL

Abram, David. The Spell of the Sensuous. New York: Vintage Books, 1997.

Ackerman, Diane. A Natural History of the Senses. New York: Vintage Books, 1990.

Ambasz, Emilio. Emilio Ambasz: The Poetics of the Pragmatic. New York: Rizzoli International, 1988.

Anderton, Frances. "Architecture for All Senses." Architectural Review 189, no. 1136 (October 1991).

Arnheim, Rudolf. The Dynamics of Architectural Form. Berkeley: University of California Press, 1977.

Bachelard, Gaston. The Poetics of Space. Boston: Beacon Press, 1969.

Barrie, T. "The Place of Architecture in the Age of Commodity." Journal of Architectural Education 49, no. 4 (1996).

Bille, M., P. Bjerregaard, and T. F. Sørensen. "Staging Atmospheres: Materiality, Culture, and the Texture of the In-Between." Emotion, Space and Society (2015).

Blesser, B., and L. R. Salter. Spaces Speak, Are You Listening? Experiencing Aural Architecture. MIT Press, 2009.

Bloomer, Kent C., and Charles W. Moore. Body, Memory, and Architecture. New Haven: Yale University Press, 1977.

Böhme, G. "Atmosphere as Mindful Physical Presence in Space." Building Atmosphere (2013).

Bonner, John Tyler. The Scale of Nature. New York: Harper & Row, 1969.

Brash, R. How Did It Begin? Superstitions and Their Romantic Origins. Australia: Longmans, Green & Co., Ltd., 1965.

Braudel, Fernand. The Structures of Everyday Life. New York: Harper & Row, 1982.

Buddenbrock, Wolfgang von. The Senses. Ann Arbor: The University of Michigan Press.

Campbell, Joseph. The Power of Myth, edited by Betty Sue Flowers, introduction by Bill Moyers. Garden City, NY: Doubleday, 1988.

Carr, Donald E. The Forgotten Senses. Garden City, NY: Doubleday, 1972.

Day, C. Places of the Soul: Architecture and Environmental Design as a Healing Art. Architectural Press, 2004.

Downing, Frances. "Memory and the Making of Places." In Ordering Space: Types in Architecture and Design, edited by Karen A. Franck and Lynda H. Schneekloth, 233. New York: Van Nostrand Reinhold, 1994.

Froman, Robert. The Many Human Senses. London: G. Bell and Sons, Ltd., 1966.

Gass, William. On Being Blue. Boston: Godine, 1976.

Gibson, James J. The Senses Considered as Perceptual Systems. Westport, CT: Greenwood Press, 1966, 1983.

Glassner, Barry. Bodies: Why We Look the Way We Do. New York: G. P. Putnam's Sons, 1988.

Goldhagen, Sarah Williams. How the Built Environment Shapes Our Lives. New York: HarperCollins, 2017.

Golledge, Reginald G. "Environmental Cognition." In Handbook of Environmental Psychology, edited by Daniel Stokols and Irwin Altman. New York: John Wiley and Sons, 1987.

Golledge, Reginald G., and Robert J. Stimson. Spatial Behavior: A Geographic Perspective. New York: Guilford Press, 1997.

Guiness, Alma E., ed. ABC's of the Human Body. Pleasantville, NY: Reader's Digest Books, 1987.

Hall, Edward T. Beyond Culture. Garden City, NY: Anchor Press/Doubleday, 1977.

Hall, Edward T. The Hidden Dimension. Garden City, NY: Anchor Books, 1969.

Haverkamp, Michael. Synesthetic Design: Handbook for a Multisensory Approach. Basel: Birkhäuser, 2013.

Heidegger, Martin. Poetry, Language, Thought, translated by Albert Hofstadter. New York: Harper and Row, 1971.

Holl, S., J. Pallasmaa, and A. Pérez-Gómez. Questions of Perception: Phenomenology of Architecture. William Stout, 2006.

Holl, Steven. "Questions of Perception: Phenomenology of Architecture." In Questions of Perception: Phenomenology of Architecture, by Steven Holl, Juhani Pallasmaa, and Alberto Pérez-Gómez. Tokyo: a + u Publishing, 1994.

Howes, D., ed. Empire of the Senses: The Sensual Culture Reader. Berg, 2005.

Howes, David, ed. Varieties of Sensory Experience: A Sourcebook in the Anthropology of the Senses. Toronto: University of Toronto Press, 1991.

Huizinga, Johan. Homo Ludens: A Study of the Play Element in Culture. Boston: Beacon Press, 1955.

Husserl, Edmund. Cartesian Meditations: An Introduction to Phenomenology, translated by Dorion Cairns. 1929; The Hague: Martinus Nijhoff, 1973.

Huysmans, J.K. Against Nature. New York: Penguin Books, 1986.

Kaplan, Stephen, and Rachel Kaplan. Cognition and Environment: Functioning in an Uncertain World. New York: Praeger Publishers, 1982.

Kaplan, Stephen, and Rachel Kaplan. The Experience of Nature: A Psychological Perspective. Cambridge: Cambridge University Press, 1989.

Köhler, Wolfgang. Gestalt Psychology. New York: Liveright, 1947.

Le Camus de Mézières, Nicolas. The Genius of Architecture, or The Analogy of That Art with Our Sensations, translated by David Britt. Santa Monica, CA: Getty Center Publication Programs, 1992.

Lipps, Andrea, and Ellen Lupton, eds. The Senses: Design Beyond Vision. United States: Princeton Architectural Press, 2018.

Martin, Russell. Matters Gray & White. New York: Fawcett/Crest, 1986.

Malnar, Joice Monice, and Frank Vodvarka. Sensory Design. Minneapolis: University of Minnesota Press, 2004.

Marks, Lawrence E. The Unity of the Senses: Interrelations among the Modalities. New York: Academic Press, 1978.

Merleau-Ponty, Maurice. Sense and Non-Sense, translated by H. L. and T. A. Dreyfus. Evanston, IL: Northwestern University Press, 1964.

Merleau-Ponty, Maurice. Phenomenology of Perception. 1945; London: Routledge and Kegan Paul, 1962.

Milne, Lorus, and Margery Milne. The Senses of Animals and Men. New York: Atheneum, 1964.

Morris, Desmond. Bodywatching. New York: Crown, 1985.

Morris, Desmond. Intimate Behavior. New York: Bantam, 1973.

Murchie, Guy. The Seven Mysteries of Life: An Exploration in Science and Philosophy. Boston: Houghton Mifflin Company, 1978.

Pallasmaa, Juhani. "Architecture of the Seven Senses." In Questions of Perception: Phenomenology of Architecture, edited by Steven Holl, Juhani Pallasmaa, and Alberto Pérez-Gómez. Tokyo: a + u Publishing, 1994.

Pallasmaa, Juhani. The Eyes of the Skin: Architecture and the Senses. West Sussex, England: John Wiley & Sons, 2012.

Panati, Charles. The Browser's Book of Beginnings. Boston: Houghton Mifflin Company, 1984.

Panati, Charles. Extraordinary Origins of Everyday Things. New York: Harper & Row, 1987.

Pearson, David. "Making Sense of Architecture." Architecture Review 10 (October 1991): Sensuality and Architecture.

Polhemus, Ted, ed. The Body Reader: Social Aspects of the Human Body. New York: Pantheon Books, 1978.

Poole, Robert M., ed. The Incredible Machine. Washington, D.C.: National Geographic Society, 1986.

Porteous, J. Douglas. Landscapes of the Mind: Worlds of Sense and Metaphor. Toronto: University of Toronto Press, 1990.

Porteous, J. Douglas. Environmental Aesthetics: Ideas, Politics, and Planning. London: Routledge, 1996.

Quantrill, Malcolm. The Environmental Memory. New York: Schocken Books, 1987.

Rasmussen, Steen Eiler. Experiencing Architecture. Cambridge: MIT Press, 1962.

Rilke, Rainer Maria. Where Silence Reigns: Selected Prose, translated by G. Craig Houston. New York: New Directions, 1978.

Rivlin, Robert, and Karen Gravelle. Deciphering the Senses: The Expanding World of Human Perception. New York: Simon & Schuster, 1984.

Robinson, Howard F., et al. Colors in the Wild. Washington, D.C.: National Wildlife Federation, 1985.

Roxo, Marcelo, et al. "The Limbic System Conception and Its Historical Evolution." Scientific World Journal 11 (2011).

Sauzet, Maurice. "Sensory Phenomena as a Reference for the Architectural Project." Architecture and Behavior 5, no. 2 (1989).

Sauzet, Maurice. "The Space of the Senses." Techniques and Architecture, July 1990.

Seamon, D. "Phenomenology, Place, Environment, and Architecture: A Review of the Literature." Eidos (2000).

Smith, Anthony. The Body. New York: Penguin Books, 1986.

Spence, Charles, and Alberto Gallace. "Multisensory Design: Reaching Out to Touch the Consumer." Psychology & Marketing 28, no. 3 (March 2011).

Synnott, Anthony. "Puzzling over the Senses: From Plato to Marx." In The Varieties of Sensory Experience: A Sourcebook in the Anthropology of the Senses, edited by David Howes. Toronto: University of Toronto Press, 1991.

Thibaud, J. P. "The Sensory Fabric of the Urban Ambiance." Ambiances. Environnement sensible, architecture et espace urbain (2015).

Thompson, D'Arcy W. On Growth and Form. Cambridge, MA: Cambridge University Press, 1961.

Twilley, Nicola. "Sight Unseen: Seeing with Your Tongue and Other Surprises of Sensory-Substitution Technology." The New Yorker, 15 May 2017.

Vitruvius, Marcus. The Ten Books on Architecture, translated by Morris Hicky Morgan. New York: Dover Publications, 1960.

Von Frisch, Karl. Animal Architecture. New York: Harcourt Brace Jovanovich, 1974.

Walsh, William S. Curiosities of Popular Customs. London: J. P. Lippincott Co., 1897.

Walter, E. V. Placeways: A Theory of the Human Environment. Chapel Hill: University of North Carolina Press, 1988.

Wilentz, Joan Steen. The Senses of Man. New York: Crowell, 1968.

Wilson, Edward O. Biophilia. Cambridge, MA: Harvard University Press, 1984.

Zumthor, P. Atmospheres: Architectural Environments – Surrounding Objects. Birkhäuser, 2006.

Zumthor, Peter. Peter Zumthor Works: Buildings and Projects, 1979-1997. Baden, Switzerland: Lars Müller Publishers, 1998.

SMELL

Akpan, Nsikan. "What a Smell Looks Like." Scientific American, 16 June 2016.

Baron, Robert A., and Marna I. Bronfen. "A Whiff of Reality: Empirical Evidence Concerning the Effects of Pleasant Fragrances on Work-Related Behavior." Journal of Applied Social Psychology 24, no. 13 (1994).

Baron, Robert A., and Jill Thomley. "A Whiff of Reality: Positive Affect as a Potential Mediator of the Effects of Pleasant Fragrances on Task Performance and Helping." Environment and Behavior 26, no. 6 (1994).

Bedichek, Roy. The Sense of Smell. Garden City, NY: Doubleday, 1960.

Bloch, Iwan. Odoratus Sexualis. New York: New York Anthropological Society, 1937.

Burton, Robert. The Language of Smell. London: Routledge & Kegan Paul, 1976.

Bushdid et al. "Humans Can Discriminate More than 1 Trillion Olfactory Stimuli." Science 343, no. 6177 (21 March 2014).

Classen, C., D. Howes, and A. Synnott. Aroma: The Cultural History of Smell. Routledge, 1994.

Clifford, C. "New Scent Waves." Self, December 1985.

Corbin, Alain. The Foul and the Fragrant. Cambridge, MA: Harvard University Press, 1986.
De Bono, K. G. "Pleasant Scents and Persuasion: An Information Processing Approach." Journal of Applied Social Psychology 22, no. 1 (1992).

Erb, Russell C. The Common Scents of Smell. New York: World Publishing Co., 1968.

Engen, Trygg. Odor Sensation and Memory. New York: Praeger Publishers, 1991.

Engen, Trygg, and Bruce M. Ross. "Long-Term Memory of Odors with and without Verbal Descriptions." Journal of Experimental Psychology 100, no. 2 (1973).

Engen, Trygg. "Remembering Odors and Their Names." American Scientist, September-October 1987.

Ferenczi, Sandor. Thalassa: Theory of Genitality. New York: W. W. Norton, 1968.

Gilbert, Avery N., Robyn Martin, and Sarah E. Kemp. "Cross-Modal Correspondence between Vision and Olfaction: The Color of Smells." American Journal of Psychology 109, no. 3 (Fall 1996).

Gilbert, A. N. What the Nose Knows: The Science of Scent in Everyday Life. Crown, 2008.

Gombrowicz, Witold. Diary, Vol. I. Evanston, IL: Northwestern University Press, 1988.

Harkness, Jack. The Makers of Heavenly Roses. London: Souvenir Press, 1985.

Henshaw, V. Urban Smellscapes: Understanding and Designing City Smell Environments. Routledge, 2014.

Henshaw, V., K. McLean, D. Medway, C. Perkins, and G. Warnaby. "Designing with Smell: Practices, Techniques and Challenges." Design Studies 52 (2017).

Johnson, Brad, Rehan M. Khan, and Noam Sobel. "Human Olfactory Psychophysics." In The Senses: A Comprehensive Reference. Amsterdam: Elsevier Academic Press, 2008.

Kemp, Sarah E., and Avery N. Gilbert. "Odor Intensity and Color Lightness Are Correlated Sensory Dimensions." American Journal of Psychology 110, no. 1 (Spring 1997).

King, J. R. "Anxiety Reduction Using Fragrances." In Perfumery: The Psychology and Biology of Fragrance. London: Chapman and Hall, 1988.

Kirk-Smith, M. D., C. Van Toller, and G. H. Dodd. "Unconscious Odour Conditioning in Human Subjects." Biological Psychology 17 (1983).

Knasko, Susan C. "Ambient Odor's Effect on Creativity, Mood, and Perceived Health." Chemical Senses 17, no. 1 (February 1992).

Lawless, Harry T. "Recognition of Common Odors, Pictures, and Simple Shapes." Perception and Psychophysics 24 (1978).

Ludvigson, H. Wayne, and Theresa R. Rottman. "Effects of Ambient Odors of Lavender and Cloves on Cognition, Memory, Affect and Mood." Chemical Senses 14, no. 4 (August 1989).

McGee, Harold. On Food and Cooking: The Science and Lure of the Kitchen. New York: Scribner, 2004.

Moncrieff, R. W. Odours. London: William Heinemann Medical Books Ltd., 1970.

Morris, Edwin T. Fragrance. New York: Scribner's, 1986.

Muller, Julia, et al. Fragrance Guide (Feminine Notes). London: Johnson Publications, n.d.

Muller, Julia, with Dr. Hans Brauer and Joachim Mensing. The H & R Book of Perfume. London: Johnson Publications.

Rabin, Michael D., and William S. Cain. "Odor Recognition: Familiarity, Identifiability, and Encoding Consistency." Journal of Experimental Psychology: Learning Memory, and Cognition 10, no. 2 (1984).

Ray, Richard, and Michael MacCarkey. Roses. Tucson, AZ: H.P. Books, 1981.

Ross, Mark, et al. "Aromas of Rosemary and Lavender Essential Oils Differentially Affect Cognition and Mood in Healthy Adults." International Journal of Neuroscience 113, no. 1 (January 2003).

Schab, Frank F. "Odor Memory: Taking Stock." Psychological Bulletin 109, no. 2 (1991).

Süskind, Patrick. Perfume. New York: Alfred A. Knopf, Inc., 1987.

Walk, Heidi A., and Elizabeth E. Johns. "Interference and Facilitation in Short-Term Memory for Odors." Perception and Psychophysics 36, no. 6 (1984).

Warm, Joel S., William N. Dember, and Raja Parasuraman. "Effects of Olfactory Stimulation on Performance and Stress in a Visual Sustained Attention Task." Journal of the Society of Cosmetic Chemists 12 (1991).

West, Paul. The Place in Flowers Where Pollen Rests. Garden City, NY: Doubleday, 1988.

Zangwill, Nick. "Aesthetic/Sensory Dependence." British Journal of Aesthetics 38, no. 1 (January 1998).

Zellner, Debra A., Angela M. Bartoli, and Robert Eckard. "Influence of Color on Odor Identification and Liking Ratings." American Journal of Psychology 104, no. 4 (Winter 1991).

TOUCH

Barker, Jennifer M. The Tactile Eye: Touch and Cinematic Experience. Berkeley: University of California Press, 2009.

Candlin, F., and R. Guins. The Object Reader. Routledge, 2009. (Contains several essays on touch and material culture)

Clark, Josh. Designing for Touch. New York: A Book Apart, 2015.

Classen, C., ed. The Book of Touch. Berg, 2005.

Classen, C. The Deepest Sense: A Cultural History of Touch. University of Illinois Press, 2012.

Cooney, Elizabeth. "Gut Feelings: Sensory Neurons Detect Fullness and Nutrients in the GI Tract in Surprising Ways." Harvard Medical School News, 26 May 2016.

Dahiya, R.S., and M. Valle. "Tactile Sensing: Definitions and Classifications." In Robotic Tactile Sensing. Dordrecht: Springer Science+Business Media, 2013.

El Saddik et al. "Haptics: General Principles." In Haptics Technologies. Berlin: Springer-Verlag, 2011.

Ernst, M. O., M. S. Banks, and H. H. Bulthof. "Haptic Feedback Affects Visual Perception of Surfaces." Perception 28, supplement (1999).

Gallico, G. Gregory, et al. "Permanent Coverage of Large Burn Wounds with Autologous Cultured Human Epithelium." The New England Journal of Medicine 311, no. 7 (August 16, 1984).

Goleman, Daniel. "The Experience of Touch: Research Points to a Critical Role." The New York Times, February 2, 1988.

Hawkins, L. H. "The Influence of Air Ions, Temperature, and Humidity on Subjective Wellbeing and Comfort." Journal of Environmental Psychology 1 (1981).

Lamb, Michael. "Second Thoughts on First Touch." Psychology Today 16, no. 4 (April 1982).

Lederman, Susan J., and Susan G. Abbott. "Texture Perception: Studies of Intersensory Organization Using a Discrepancy Paradigm, and Visual Versus Tactual Psychophysics." Journal of Experimental Psychology: Human Perception and Performance 7, no. 4 (1981).

Linden, David J. Touch: The Science of Hand, Heart, and Mind. New York: Viking, 2015.

Lebeck, Robert. The Kiss. New York: St. Martin's Press, 1981.

Lupton, Ellen. Skin: Surface, Substance + Design. New York: Cooper-Hewitt, National Design Museum and Princeton Architectural Press, 2012.

Macrae, Janet. Therapeutic Touch: A Practical Guide. New York: Alfred A. Knopf, Inc., 1988.

Miller, Meg. "The Complicated Quest to Redesign Braille." Co.Design, 28 September 2017.

Montagu, Ashley. Touching: The Human Significance of the Skin. New York: Harper & Row, 1986.

Palmer, Riitta Lahtinen Russ. "History of Social-Haptic Communication." Paper presented at the 4th European Deafblind Conference, Espoo, Finland, 1996.

Paterson, M. The Senses of Touch: Haptics, Affects and Technologies. Berg, 2007.

Sachs, Frederick. "The Intimate Sense of Touch." The Sciences, January/February 1988.

Spence, Charles, and Alberto Gallace. "Multisensory Design: Reaching Out to Touch the Consumer." Psychology & Marketing 28, no. 3 (March 2011).

TASTE

Brillat-Savarin, Anthelme. The Physiology of Taste, translated and annotated by M. F. K. Fisher. San Francisco, CA: North Point Press, 1999.

C. Bushdid, M. O. Magnasco, L. B. Vosshall, and A. Keller. "Humans Can Discriminate More than 1 Trillion Olfactory Stimuli." Science 343, no. 6177 (2014).

Farb, Peter, and George Armelagos. Consuming Passions. New York: Washington Square Press, 1970.

Harrar, Vanessa, Betina Piqueras-Fiszman, and Charles Spence. "There's More to Taste in a Coloured Bowl." Perception 40 (2011).

Harris, Marvin. The Sacred Cow and the Abominable Pig: Riddles of Food and Culture. New York: Simon & Schuster/Touchstone Books, 1987.

Korsmeyer, C. Making Sense of Taste: Food and Philosophy. Cornell University Press, 2002.

Liebowitz, Michael. The Chemistry of Love. New York: Berkeley Books, 1984.

Piqueras-Fiszmana, Betina, Vanessa Harrar, Jorge Alcaide, and Charles Spence. "Does the Weight of the Dish Influence Our Perception of Food?" Food Quality and Preference 22, no. 8 (2011).

Prescott, J. Taste Matters: Why We Like the Foods We Do. Reaktion Books, 2015.

Shepherd, Gordon M. Neurogastronomy: How the Brain Creates Flavor and Why It Matters. New York: Columbia University Press, 2017.

Spence, C. Tasty: The Art and Science of What We Eat. Scribner, 2020.

Spence, Charles, Carmel A. Levitan, Maya U. Shankar, and Massimiliano Zampini. "Does Food Color Influence Taste and Flavor Perception in Humans?" Chemosensory Perception 3, no. 1 (2010).

Spence, Charles. "Sound: The Forgotten Flavor Sense." In Multisensory Flavor Perception: From Fundamental Neuroscience through to the Marketplace, edited by Betina Piqueras-Fiszman and Charles Spence. Cambridge, MA: Woodhead Publishing, 2016.

Velasco, Carlos, Andy T. Woods, Lawrence E. Marks, Adrian David Cheok, and Charles Spence. "The Semantic Basis of Taste-Shape Associations." Psychiatry and Psychology 4 (2016).

Wansink, Brian. "Environmental Factors That Increase the Food Intake and Consumption Volume of Unknowing Consumers." Annual Review of Nutrition 24 (2004).

SOUND

Anwar, Yasmin. "Back to the Blues, Our Emotions Match Music to Colors." Berkeley News, 16 May 2013.

Attali, Jacques. Noise: The Political Economy of Music, translated by Brian Massumi. Minneapolis: University of Minnesota Press, 1985.

Beckerman, Joel. Sonic Boom: How Sound Transforms the Way We Think, Feel, and Buy. New York: Houghton Mifflin Harcourt, 2014.

Broad, William J. "Complex Whistles Found to Play Key Roles in Inca and Maya Life." The New York Times, March 29, 1988.

Chatwin, Bruce. The Songlines. New York: The Viking Press, 1987.

Cooke, Deryck. The Language of Music. London: Oxford University Press, 1987.

Cox, C. "Beyond Representation and Signification: Toward a Sonic Materialism." Journal of Visual Culture 12, no. 2 (2013).

Farnell, Andy. Designing Sound. Cambridge: MIT Press, 2010.

Grant, Brian. The Silent Ear: Deafness in Literature. New York: Faber and Faber, 1988.

Sterne, J. The Audible Past: Cultural Origins of Sound Reproduction. Duke University Press, 2003.

Miller, Melinda. "How Does Acoustical Absorption Work?" Acoustics by Design, 8 December 2011.

Paul, Peter V. Toward a Psychology of Deafness: Theoretical and Empirical Perspectives. MA: Allyn & Bacon, 1993.

Schaeffer, R. Murray. "Acoustic Space." In Dwelling, Place, and Environment: Towards a Phenomenology of Person and World, edited by David Seamon and Robert Mugerauer. Boston: Martinus Nijhoff, 1985.

Schaeffer, R. Murray. The Composer in the Classroom. Toronto: Clark and Cruickshank, 1965.

Schaeffer, R. Murray. The Tuning of the World. New York: Alfred A. Knopf, 1977.

Schonberg, Harold. Facing the Music. New York: Summit Books, 1985.

Southworth, Michael. "The Sonic Environment of Cities." Environment and Behavior, June 1969.

Stambler, Irwin. The World of Sounds. New York: W. W. Norton, 1967.

Till, R. "Architectural Soundscapes: Building Performance and Acoustic Space." Architectural Design 80, no. 3 (2010).

Truax, B. Acoustic Communication. Springer Science & Business Media, 2012.

TIME

Glicksohn, Joseph. "Subjective Time Estimation in Altered Sensory Environments." Environment and Behavior 24 (September 1992).

Leiser, David, Eliahu Stern, and Joachim Meyer. "Mean Velocity and Total Time Estimation Effects of Order and Proportions." Journal of Environmental Psychology 11 (1991).

Zakay, D., D. Nitzan, and J. Glocksohn. "The Influence of Task Difficulty and External Tempo on Subjective Time Estimation." Perception and Psychophysics 34 (1983).

VISION

Bataille, Georges. Story of the Eye, translated by J. Neugroschal. San Francisco: City Lights Books, 1987.

Bataille, Georges. Visions of Excess: Selected Writings 1927-1939, translated by Allen Stockl. Minneapolis: University of Minneapolis Press, 1985.

Berger, John. About Looking. New York: Pantheon Books, 1980.

Berger, John. The Sense of Sight. New York: Pantheon Books, 1980.

Bova, Ben. The Beauty of Light. New York: John Wiley & Sons, Inc., 1988.

Citowic, Richard E., and David M. Eagleman. Wednesday Is Indigo Blue: Discovering the Brain of Synesthesia. Cambridge, MA: MIT Press, 2009.

Crary, J. Techniques of the Observer: On Vision and Modernity in the Nineteenth Century. MIT Press, 1992.

Hård, Anders. "The Natural Colour System and Its Universal Application in the Study of Environmental Design." In Colour for Architecture, edited by Tom Porter and Byron Mikellides. London: Studio Vista, 1976.

Heerwagen, Judith H. "Affective Functioning, 'Light Hunger,' and Room Brightness Preferences." Environment and Behavior 22 (September 1990).

Ittelson, William H. Visual Space Perception. New York: Springer, 1960.

Itten, Johannes. The Elements of Color: A Treatise on the Color System of Johannes Itten Based on His Book 'The Art of Color', edited by Faber Birren, translated by Ernst Van Hagen. New York: Van Nostrand Reinhold, 1970.

Jay, M. Downcast Eyes: The Denigration of Vision in Twentieth-Century French Thought. University of California Press, 1994.

Koretz, Jane F., and George H. Handelman. "How the Human Eye Focuses." Scientific American, July 1988.

Lauwereyns, Jan. Brain and the Gaze: On the Active Boundaries of Vision. Cambridge, MA: MIT Press, 2012.

Mahnke, Frank H., and Rudolf H. Mahnke. Color and Light in Man-Made Environments. New York: Van Nostrand Reinhold, 1987.

Millet, Marietta S. Light Revealing Architecture. New York: Van Nostrand Reinhold, 1996.
Molnar, François. "A Science of Vision for Visual Art." In Emerging Visions of the Aesthetic Process: Psychology, Semiology, and Philosophy, edited by Gerald C. Cupchik and János László. Cambridge: Cambridge University Press, 1992.

Nicolaides, Kimon. The Natural Way to Draw: A Working Plan for Art Study. Boston: Houghton Mifflin Company, 1941.

Passini, Romedi. Wayfinding in Architecture. 1984; New York: Van Nostrand Reinhold, 1992.

Piaget, Jean. The Mechanisms of Perception, translated by G. N. Seagrim. 1961; New York: Basic Books, 1969.

Rossotti, Hazel. Colour: Why the World Isn't Grey. Princeton, NJ: Princeton University Press, 1983.

Segall, Marshall H., Donald T. Campbell, and Melville J. Herskovits. The Influence of Culture on Visual Perception: An Advanced Study in Psychology and Anthropology. Indianapolis: Bobbs-Merrill, 1966.

Sekiguchi, H., and H. Nakayama. "On a History and a Present Circumstances of Walking for Persons with Visual Impairments in Japan." Paper presented at the 5th International Conference on Civil Engineering, 29-31 August 2002, Manila, Philippines.

Sharpe, Deborah T. The Psychology of Color and Design. Totowa, NJ: Littlefield, Adams, 1981.

Stafford, B. M. Visual Analogy: Consciousness as the Art of Connecting. MIT Press, 1999.

Taylor, Ashley P. "Newton's Color Theory, ca. 1665." The Scientist, 1 March 2017.

Taylor, Joshua C. Learning to Look: A Handbook for the Visual Arts. Chicago, IL: University of Chicago Press, 1957.

Trevor-Roper, Patrick. The World Through Blunted Sight. London: Penguin Books, 1988.

Tuan, Yi-Fu. Space and Place: The Perspective of Experience. Minneapolis: University of Minnesota Press, 1977.

Tufte, Edward R. Envisioning Information. Cheshire, CT: Graphics Press, 1990.

Valdez, Patricia, and Albert Mehrabian. "Effects of Color on Emotion." Journal of Experimental Psychology 123, no. 4 (1994).

Vaughan, Christopher. "A New View of Vision." Science News, July 23, 1988.

Wilson, Forrest. A Graphic Survey of Perception and Behavior for the Design Professions. New York: Van Nostrand Reinhold, 1984.

Wurm, Lee H., et al. "Color Improves Object Recognition in Normal and Low Vision." Journal of Experimental Psychology: Human Perception and Performance 19, no. 4 (1993).

Zellner, Debra A. "Color-Odor Interactions: A Review and Model." Chemosensory Perception 6, no. 4 (December 2013).